COLLECTED ARTICLES ON GEORGE GISSING

GEORGE GISSING

Illustrated London News May 1 1897

Collected Articles on GEORGE GISSING

Edited by

PIERRE COUSTILLAS

LONDON AND NEW YORK

First published 1968 by Frank Cass and Company Limited

2 Park Square, Milton Park, Abingdon, Oxon OX14 4RN
711 Third Avenue, New York, NY 10017, USA

Routledge is an imprint of the Taylor & Francis Group, an informa business

First issued in paperback 2016

ISBN 978-0-7146-2054-1 (hbk)
ISBN 978-1-138-97107-3 (pbk)

Contents

PART THREE—SOME VIEWS ON THE MAJOR WORKS

Introduction

IN the English literary production of the eighteen eighties and nineties, George Gissing stands as an important figure. A younger contemporary of Meredith and Hardy, he has always had a smaller following, but from the publication of his first books to the present day his name has roused the enthusiastic support of a tenaciously faithful minority. Yet his life and works have occasionally called from 'superior' critics judgments which, if assembled, would seem to condemn him to oblivion. But Time alone is doing him justice. *He* remains whereas his most unperceptive and ill-natured censors—William McFee in the forefront of these—have cried out their incomprehension and sunk into silence. Now that his achievements have ceased to excite passion and controversy, his contribution to English fiction can be viewed with objectivity. The rising interest in him since the centenary of his birth in 1957 is efficiently consolidating his very substantial claim to be reckoned as a significant novelist of the late Victorian period.

He was in revolt against his time and though his artistic integrity told severely upon his earnings, he protested until the very end against social abuses, vulgar pretentiousness and false attitudes of all kinds. His pessimism which very much irked his contemporaries sworn to a sanguine view of life, however widely it may have been contradicted by mere observation, has a distinct flavour, a personal note which makes his books so unmistakably his own. It always renders the correlation of his biography and his fiction illuminating for both. For indeed his existence was ill-starred.

His earliest misfortune occurred in 1870 when, at the age of thirteen, he lost his father, a pharmaceutical chemist and botanist of local note. George, who was the eldest of five children, was then sent with his two brothers to a boarding school at Alderley Edge in Cheshire. There he gave brilliant proof of his intellectual abilities, and he seemed to have a future already cut out when, two years later, he came out first for the whole of England in the Oxford Local examination, a feat that was rewarded by a scholarship at Owens College, Manchester. Unfortunately, in the winter of 1875-76, whereas he went on winning the highest academic distinctions, he became infatuated with a seventeen-year-old girl of the streets, Marianne Helen Harrison. With the generosity and illusions of youth, he set his mind on redeeming her, considering that society alone was responsible for her misadventure. He tried to bring her back to a decent life, gave her as much of his own money as he could spare and even bought her a sewing-machine that she might earn her livelihood by honest means. When his own resources were exhausted, he committed a series of thefts in the College, which eventually led to his being caught by the police. He was immediately expelled, brought to justice and sentenced to one month's imprisonment with hard labour. Thus it was that his distinguished student's career came to an end.

Some friends of his deceased father arranged for his migrating to America in the hope that he would make a new start in life, but he failed to get a foothold. Threatened by starvation, he spontaneously turned to fiction for a living and never after altered his purpose. Like his semi-autobiographical character Henry Ryecroft, he became 'a struggling man, beset by poverty and other circumstances very unpropitious to mental work'. On returning from the States, in the autumn of 1877, he sought the girl of the streets for whom he had forfeited his honour. They lived for a time together, then he married her, but all his efforts to reclaim her were vain; she became an inveterate drinker and returned to her trade. After some years of infernal matrimony, they separated. She died in a Lambeth slum in February 1888.

Nor was his second union three years later, with a working-class girl, any happier. He married her on account of a certain form of masochism and in order to avoid sexual starvation, but marriage soon revealed the incompatibility of their tempers—the quiet, submissive Edith turned into a shrew, insulted her husband and beat her son. Of the years they spent in common his novel *In the Year of Jubilee* offers an oblique, yet vivid picture. But for his son, to whom he was deeply attached, Gissing would have left his wife after a couple of years; he tried to be patient, humoured her as best he could and even accepted a reconciliation after a temporary separation in the spring of 1897. But the crisis came to a head a few months later. When his patience was strained to the breaking-point, he fled to Italy, where his work would not be daily interrupted by domestic explosions. He never saw his wife again. She had eventually to be sent to a lunatic asylum.

Only towards the end of his life did he enjoy comparative happiness with a young French lady whose acquaintance he had made through her request to translate *New Grub Street.* In Gabrielle Fleury he at last found the intellectual equal he had dreamt to conquer as a wife. As ill luck would have it, divorce from Edith proved impossible and he could not marry Gabrielle, a situation which cast a shadow over his last years. Though he was then partly relieved of financial cares by the greater proceeds from his books, his years in France were also saddened by declining health. He died at Ispoure, near Saint-Jean-Pied-de-Port, on December 28, 1903. The French Pyrenees had been the last stage of his pathetic quest of a suitable climate. In more senses than one he died in exile.

His complete works will, when collected, amount to some twenty-five or thirty volumes consisting mainly of fiction—novels and short stories—criticism of Dickens, a book of travel and various essays best represented by *The Private Papers of Henry Ryecroft.* Most of these works cry for reprinting, and there is some hope that a selection of the novels will reappear before long. The student of Gissing will find three full-length biographies available. The earliest one, *The Private Life of Henry Maitland*, by Morley Roberts, the author's friend from his student's days, is a *roman à clef*, deplorable in tone, patronising and full of inaccuracies in detail. Minutely edited, it would still be very useful. Morchard Bishop's critical edition of it (Richards Press, 1958) corrects some mistakes and gives a key to the pseudonyms but leaves dozens of errors and inconsistencies unnoted. Mabel C. Donnelly's *George Gissing: Grave Comedian* (1954) is objective enough but remains superficial and patchy. It is now superseded by Jacob Korg's *George Gissing: A Critical Biography* (University of Washington Press, 1963; Methuen, 1965). At present, at least two other biographies are being prepared.

Gissing's correspondence includes, beside two very scarce booklets containing some letters to Edward Clodd and Clement Shorter, *The Letters of George Gissing to Members of his Family* (1927), bowdlerized but indispensable, *George Gissing and H. G. Wells, Their Friendship and Correspondence*, ed. Royal A. Gettmann (University of Illinois Press and Rupert Hart-Davis, 1961), *The Letters of George Gissing to Eduard Bertz 1887-1903*, ed. Arthur C. Young (Rutgers University Press and Constable, 1961) and *The Letters of George Gissing to Gabrielle Fleury*, ed. Pierre Coustillas (The New York Public Library, 1964).

Among the critical studies Frank Swinnerton's *George Gissing* (1912) was the first to appear. It was published in the same year as

Roberts's fictionalized biography and its tone is about as deplorable; Swinnerton's carping, his quasi systematic attempt to belittle his subject have, since the book's publication, infuriated the novelist's friends and admirers. Gissing was avenged by Ruth Capers McKay in her *George Gissing and His Critic Frank Swinnerton* (1933). Another general survey, *George Gissing: An Appreciation*, by May Yates came out in 1922. Samuel Vogt Gapp devoted a whole well-informed book to *George Gissing, Classicist* (1936). Since that date a number of excellent articles have appeared but no book-length appraisement, although several are expected to appear in the next few years. Investigation of late has rather borne on definite biographical areas such as Gissing's relations with important friends and publishers. Up to 1961, the Gissing student will find a good general survey of the critical work on the author in *Victorian Fiction* (Harvard, 1964); in a dozen pages, Jacob Korg has covered the most significant publications.

Bibliographies describing the first editions will be found in Henry Danielson's *Bibliographies of Modern Authors* (1921), in the posthumously published *Critical Studies of the Works of Charles Dickens*, by Gissing (1924), and in Dr. Jacob Schwartz's *1,100 Obscure Points* (1931). Lists of abstracted articles have occasionally been issued in *English Fiction* (afterwards *English Literature*) *in Transition*, specially vol. I, nos. 2 and 3 (1957-58), vol. III, no. 2 (1960), vol. VII, nos. 1 and 2 (1964), vol. VIII, no. 5 (1965). A bibliography of Gissing's short stories is also to be found in the same periodical in vol. VII, no. 2 (1964). For current articles and books the reader is naturally referred to the annual bibliographies of *PMLA* and *Victorian Studies*.

In the following selection of essays, stress has been laid almost exclusively on criticism, but biographical clues are frequently given in the pieces reprinted. It will be seen in the footnotes recording their source that they were not all articles originally, but their interest is certainly not affected thereby. The limitation of 'views on major works' to six, dealing in fact with four books, may at first seem regrettable, but the index, pointing to judgments on all Gissing's works in the other pieces shows that some compensation is offered. Whereas I wish I could have used John Middleton Murry's thoughtful essay on the novelist's feminine portraiture had it not been so copious, I do not think it necessary to apologize for the inclusion of three studies by Jacob Korg. With Arthur C. Young, whose contributions to the literature on the author have so far dealt with biographical aspects, he has helped to make the Gissing revival a plain fact. My sole desire is that the present anthology may bring new students into touch with the novelist's works. The field to be covered is large and the harvest sure to be stimulating.

GISSING'S WORKS

The place of publication, except when otherwise stated, is London. Only the first edition is listed together with the earliest revised edition when any. Of all the books published in his lifetime and immediately after his death, *Isabel Clarendon* is the only one which was never reprinted.

1880 *Workers in the Dawn*. 3 vols. Remington & Co. (a two-volume edition recording the alterations projected by Gissing for the first volume, was introduced and annotated by Robert Shafer for Doubleday, Doran & Co. of New York in 1935).
1884 *The Unclassed*. 3 vols. Chapman & Hall (revised edition, 1 vol., Lawrence & Bullen, 1895).
1886 *Demos*. 3 vols. Smith, Elder.
1886 *Isabel Clarendon*. 2 vols. Chapman & Hall.
1887 *Thyrza*. 3 vols. Smith, Elder (revised edition, 1 vol. Smith, Elder, 1891).
1888 *A Life's Morning*. 3 vols. Smith, Elder.
1889 *The Nether World*. 3 vols. Smith, Elder.
1890 *The Emancipated*. 3 vols. Bentley & Son (revised edition, 1 vol., Lawrence & Bullen, 1893).
1891 *New Grub Street*. 3 vols. Smith, Elder.
1892 *Denzil Quarrier*. Lawrence & Bullen.
1892 *Born in Exile*. 3 vols. A & C. Black.
1893 *The Odd Women*. 3 vols. Lawrence & Bullen.
1894 *In the Year of Jubilee*. 3 vols. Lawrence & Bullen.
1895 *Eve's Ransom*. Lawrence & Bullen.
1895 *Sleeping Fires*. Fisher, Unwin.
1895 *The Paying Guest*. Cassell & Co.
1897 *The Whirlpool*. Lawrence & Bullen.

1898 *Human Odds & Ends*. Lawrence & Bullen (short stories).
1898 *Charles Dickens: A Critical Study*. Blackie & Son (revised edition, Gresham Publishing Company, 1902).
1898 *The Town Traveller*. Methuen & Co.
1899 *The Crown of Life*. Methuen & Co.
1901 *Our Friend the Charlatan*. Chapman & Hall.
1901 *By the Ionian Sea*. Chapman & Hall.
1903 Forster's *Life* of Charles Dickens, revised and abridged. Chapman & Hall.
1903 *The Private Papers of Henry Ryecroft*. Constable & Co.
1904 *Veranilda*. Constable & Co.
1905 *Will Warburton*. Constable & Co.
1906 *The House of Cobwebs*. Constable & Co. With an introductory survey by Thomas Seccombe (short stories).
1924 *The Sins of the Fathers and Other Tales*. Chicago: Pascal Covici. With an introduction by Vincent Starrett (four of the early American short stories).
1924 *Critical Studies of the Works of Charles Dickens*. New York: Greenberg. With an introduction and bibliography by Temple Scott.
1925 *The Immortal Dickens*. Cecil Palmer (this volume, like the previous one, contains nine of the original introductions by Gissing for the Rochester edition of Dickens's works).
1927 *A Victim of Circumstances*. Constable & Co. (short stories). With an introduction by A. C. Gissing.
1929 *Selections Autobiographical & Imaginative from the Works of George Gissing*. Jonathan Cape. Ed. A. C. Gissing. Introduction by Virginia Woolf.
1931 *Brownie*. New York: Columbia University Press. (Seven of the early American short stories). With introductions by G. E. Hastings, V. Starrett and T. O. Mabbott.
1938 *Stories and Sketches*. Michael Joseph. With an introduction by A. C. Gissing.
1962 *George Gissing's Commonplace Book*. Ed. Jacob Korg. The New York Public Library.

Fresnes 1967 PIERRE COUSTILLAS

PART ONE

General Studies

1

*Who Knows George Gissing?**

Russell Kirk

About Wakefield, in West Riding, lies what we might call the Gissing country. Ride the circuit of this interminable chain of mill towns —Leeds, Bradford, Halifax, Dewsbury, Wakefield—with their halo of smutty mist, their dismal walls of soiled stone or half-brick, their desolation of slack-jawed streets, and one may reflect that they seem ingeniously designed for the torment of any man who cares for beauty and tradition. Wakefield, which of them all appears most nearly heartless, has a fine parish church (now a cathedral) built six hundred years before George Gissing came into the world; and it has a decent public library, established some years after he died; otherwise, it is one of Cobbett's hell-holes. On a principal street, opposite 'Betty's Snack Bar', à la U.S.A., is rather an old brick house of three stories, one of the few buildings in the city that can claim even Georgian venerability. The ground floor is a chemist's shop, a unit in the great chain of Boots, Ltd. In 1857, there was a chemist's shop in the same place—the establishment of a scholarly pharmacist named Gissing. In that year, a brass plate at the door records, was born in the room above the shop George Gissing, 'novelist and man of letters'. The automobiles honk past the house in the ugly road.

I

Fifty years ago, early in 1900, George Gissing was beginning to die at the age of forty-three; he had left England for the Continent, to spend in France nearly the whole of what remained to him of life. With him was his Gabrielle, whom he could not make his wife, for the fate that spoiled all his loves followed him to the end. When

* Reprinted from the *Western Humanities Review*, Summer 1950, pp. 213-22, by permission of the editors.

hardly more than a boy, he had half relished the idea of a life like one of Murger's Bohemians; very nearly such a life, or its English counterpart, had been his; and it had been a long curse of poverty and solitude. Few people ever had read his books; now, he feared, these few were commencing to forget him; and it was to supply the means of existence in the shadow of the Pyrenees that he finished the book which was to bring him, dead, the reputation he had coveted in his London garrets and cellars: *The Private Papers of Henry Ryecroft*. Of this, the novelist wrote that it was 'the thing most likely to last when all my other futile work has followed my futile life'. The twentieth century had arrived—1900, of which he had said to his brother two decades before: 'That year ought to be fertile in great things.' Gissing had altered; and when the year was come indeed, he now told a friend, 'The barbarization of the world goes merrily on. No doubt there will be continuous warfare for many a long year. It sickens me to read the newspapers; I turn as much as possible to the old poets.' First he had wanted to be the reformer of society, and later to be the servant of art; and he ended as the connoisseur of misery.

Dead half a century, nearly! To the reader of *Ryecroft* or *New Grub Street*, this is a curious thought, for in Gissing's pages lives the sense of an evening's conversation, an exchange of opinions with a contemporary, the voice of a conscience speaking to a conscience. Older authors there are, from whose books comes the same illusion —Plutarch, for one; but they are not many. And, then, Gissing died young; comrades of his, like H. G. Wells, were with us only yesterday. Having read something of Gissing's, one feels that he would really have liked to know the man. Perhaps the glow of intellectual fellowship that seems to emanate from Gissing is a reflection of a chief pleasure of Gissing's own, good talk of people and books with men who understand. Certainly he got little pleasure from the sources of satisfaction which generally rank high—fine houses, good food, loving women—dearly though he coveted these, too. One glimpses a genuine manliness in Gissing, a manliness transcending the flaws of character he recognized in himself, a manliness of which many a literary figure of the past seventy years could have used a share.

Yet quite dead, and buried at St. Jean de Luz, and rightly so, this man with whom one would have liked to talk. There is about Gissing's career the fitness which is stamped upon the classical models he reverenced. It was fit that he should labour for a pittance, and fit that he should die abroad, brooding and exhausted, at a time when most men are only beginning to master life. It seems as fit in Gissing as it does in all his better stories, for he was a species of incarnation of protest against the modern temper. Remorselessly true, in his novels, to the candid observation of human nature, this Gissing: the naïve enthusiast is baffled, the rebel wearied or corrupted, the weakling broken. Just so was he uncompromisingly true to his own character. Having commenced as a Quixote, he clung stubbornly, even when the mists of youth had drifted away from his eyes, to an ideal of life and work that he would not abandon. Can we imagine a successful Gissing, writing to please Mr. Mudie's subscribers, holding the admiration of Amy Reardon, aping his own Jasper Milvain? Can we even imagine him tranquil as Ryecroft? He lived and died as it befitted a man of his ideals to endure and perish, and that without a drop of the heavy dose of *poseur* which infected so many writers of his generation—Moore, Wilde, Rimbaud. Thus the story of Gissing is better than any of his novels, all of which were patches ripped from the Nessus' shirt of his existence.

A moving story, Gissing's life, but a story not many know except for rags and tatters of scandal and sentimental commiseration. The public for which Gissing wrote, and the admirers of his talent since his death, always were few. Once, visiting a family of teachers in Bradford, close to the scenes of Gissing's boyhood, I mentioned that I was going to Wakefield to photograph Gissing's house. Who was Gissing? my hosts wanted to know; and, on being told, what sort of thing did he write? These were people of some schooling, of as much schooling as Gissing himself had; but I was not surprised. On the other hand, one afternoon in a prosperous bookshop in San Francisco I came upon old copies of two novels of Gissing's which, like most of his, are hard to find; and presenting these at the cashier's counter, I found myself envied by the clerk, who would have taken them for himself had he known they were in the shop. The scattered confraternity of those who really know Gissing, is conspicuous not for size, but for sincerity and persistence of esteem. The man had something in him, thus to find his way obscurely into odd corners of society and stick there.

At intervals a flurry of renewed attention to Gissing's books and character breaks into print. One such commotion followed close upon his death; another, after the publication in 1912 of those two curious, condescending books *The Private Life of Henry Maitland* and *George Gissing, a Critical Study*; a third, at the time of the republication of both those volumes, 1923. In this year, even his best-known books, except for *Ryecroft,* are out of print in America and Britain; but presently they will return to booksellers' shelves, for a regular, though subtle, demand induces new editions.

What manner of man remembers Gissing? Frank Swinnerton, whose chief, but convincing, tribute to Gissing is imitation, would have us think that 'ill-educated egoists', and such only, are Gissing's devotees. Now, it is quite true that many of the quarter-educated at whom Gissing himself so often scoffed are drawn to that literary naturalism which in part descends from Gissing; but these people—many of them young and only commencing a general acquaintance with literature—do not today seek out Gissing. Indeed, they have not heard of him at all; they sport about the feet of Wolfe and Farrell and Dreiser or some other idol, writers for them more attractive precisely because, whatever their merits, the Wolfes and Dreisers and Farrells of our time have themselves been ill-educated and egoistic. Gissing, on the contrary, was educated all too thoroughly, if such a thing be possible, supported throughout life by the classical discipline; and if egoism means self-conceit, he had hardly any of it. A realistic novelist who does not blame circumstance or environment or heredity for his failures hardly seems conceivable, here in the middle of the twentieth century. But Gissing did not. He blamed his own character.

I am inclined to think that most people who still read Gissing, far from being ill-educated egoists, are generous, contemplative, conservative, liberal (for the latter two terms need not exclude one another). Most of them had their attention first drawn to him by being told of *Henry Ryecroft,* and having passed beyond that noble little book into the sombre depths of the novels, never managed to forget him. I may be in error concerning Gissing-readers, not having interviewed a truly random sample, to employ a phrase repugnant to the Gissing tradition; for although I have talked with some hundreds of people who read books, I have met with very few who know George Gissing.

One reason why so few make his acquaintance lies in the fitting circumstance that Gissing, unfortunate in his choice of occupations and women, seems often to have been no more fortunate in his choice of friends. The principal accounts of his private life come from two literary men who were close to Gissing while he lived, but who dealt with him chiefly in superior pity once he was dead: Morley Roberts and H. G. Wells. Compare Gissing's treatment of Wells in

Ryecroft ('G. H. Rivers', you may remember)[1] with Wells' treatment of Gissing in *Experiment in Autobiography*, and you shiver at the thought of what can be done to you once you are fled from this vile world. Another reason is that Mrs. Grundy, whom Gissing more than once defied by name and defeated (in Pyrrhic style), exults over him now that he is dead, and fear of what that woman might say has induced people who loved him to lock up letters and choose their phrases. Gissing ought to be indemnified for both injuries.

II

Known to fewer than he ought to be, George Gissing; but known, still. What has saved him from the abyss into which slipped the welter of late-Victorian and Edwardian novelists? Not the mere distinction of having been the first man to write accurately of the nether world. His soul saved him; and his expression of modern pessimism; besides his modern version of the consolations of Epicurus; and certain rare merits as a literary artist. These properties have kept him afloat on the literary sea and may suffice to buoy him up even after certain reputations of his generation still prominent have gone under.

He has kept afloat; he has continued to interest critics of high talents; but somehow his admirers always write of him half apologetically, as if it were necessary to dampen their own praise. This trait begins with Gissing's obituary in the London *Times* of 1903: 'The result was a series of books which, if they cannot justly be called great, were at least the work of a very able and conscientious artist, whose purity and solidity may win him a better chance of being read a hundred years hence than many writers of greater grace and more deliberately sought charm.' Paul Elmer More, in 1918: 'Gissing has his devotees, of whom, to a certain extent, I count myself one. But none of us, I think, would place him quite on a level with Thackeray and Trollope.' Granville Hicks, in 1939: 'Gissing's achievement . . . though it was repeatedly marred by defects of an uncommon grossness, was substantial.'

The confirmed Gissing-reader knows what these critics mean. Gissing, compelled to pay homage to the publishers' three-volume novel, often was prolix; sometimes he was oddly stiff in his beginning

[1] A confusion. In *The Private Papers of Henry Ryecroft* (Summer XXIII) Gissing referred to Wells as N—. G. H. Rivers is the pseudonym Morley Roberts used for Wells in *The Private Life of Henry Maitland*. (P. C. 1967.)

chapter; now and then, the strong effect he achieves near the middle of his story trickles away before *finis*. One feels these things sorrowfully. But then, perhaps, a reaction commences in the judgment of the Gissing-reader, who proceeds to ask himself just why he experienced this dissatisfaction. Could it have been because Gissing came so near to creating the illusion of reality that his failure to accomplish the whole of the sorcery told the more painfully? We do not expect from most important English novelists a complete reproduction of life—certainly not from Hardy or Meredith, Gissing's contemporaries. We do expect it from Gissing, because it is the goal he set himself. Prolix, stiff, uneven he is, on occasion. But is not Trollope more digressive? Hardy sometimes more formal? Dickens less balanced? The Gissing-reader is tempted to remark to himself, 'Gissing may not be in the first rank of novelists. But who is?'

A Gissing-reader often has difficulty in determining whether he is attracted by Gissing's books or by Gissing's soul. In the Christian sense, Gissing—metempsychosed Epicurean that he was—hardly would have acknowledged the possession of a soul; but, tormented, it bobs up before us. The interesting characteristic of this soul is its defiance of circumstance. Plunged among the poorest of the poor, he rises to scoff at equality and social revolution; subjected to repeated injuries at the hands of women, he idealizes Woman; engulfed by industrialism, he finds his home in Greece and Rome; reared in materialism, he becomes a partisan of morality. Whatever his misadventures, the man who possessed this soul was either strong or perverse.

His was a soul aching with the pessimism of our time. In the dreariness of modern life, in the melancholy expression of alarm at the death of old ways, in the wail of the inhabitants of the metropolitan nether world, in the self-probing inspection of the vanity of human wishes, in the preoccupation with amorous passion and with the problems of marriage that are so much with us now—in these themes of Gissing's is contained an analysis of our miseries no writer since has surpassed. The artist of misery can never be popular; but, having genius, neither can he be forgotten.

III

Unlike many other realistic novelists, Gissing was a true artist. He began as a pamphleteer; but soon abandoning the crusade for social reform, he made artistic beauty his life's aim—the beauty of truth, barren, perhaps, yet always dignified by literary style of a high order. His Harold Biffen stalks after a butcher and his girl, alert to record their every phrase; but such was not really Gissing's own method. The fascination with trivia, the gloating over psychological detail, the sobersided imitation of sociology that have come to be identified with realism are not found in Gissing; Stephen Crane is a cataloguer beside him, Frank Norris a dust-sifter. Reality, he was determined to reproduce, but reality chiefly of human character, delineated against a sketchy background of the commonplace details of life. To accomplish his purpose he possessed a tool denied his twentieth-century inheritors: the discipline of classical thought and letters. Few other Englishmen have been so much in love with the books and traditions of Greece and Rome as was this poverty-spurred young man from industrial Yorkshire; what few pounds he could save during his literary slaving were spent to take him to Italy and Athens. With the classical tradition he combined a minute knowledge of English authors, so that the models for his style were Scott and Thackeray and Dickens, not Turgenev and Dostoevsky and Balzac, admirer of the Continental realists though he became; he presents no parallel with George Moore's imitation of Zola. His school of literary realism was of his own foundation, a growth out of his early miseries in the depths of London.

Accordingly, in these remorseless tales of his is a literary beauty—a union that has come to be thought anomalous in naturalistic fiction. Take a single passage of description from *Thyrza* (chosen not because it is markedly striking, but because it is a good sample of Gissing's pace)—realism unadulterated, but the realism of a man with taste and discrimination:

> Caledonian Road is a great channel of traffic running directly north from King's Cross to Holloway. It is doubtful whether London can show any thoroughfare of importance more offensive to eye and ear and nostril. You stand at the entrance to it, and gaze into a region of supreme ugliness; every house front is marked with meanness and inveterate grime; every shop seems breaking forth with mould or dry-rot; the people who walk here appear one and all to be employed in labour that soils body and mind. Journey on the top of a tram-car from King's Cross to Holloway, and civilization has taught you its ultimate achievement in ignoble hideousness. You look off into narrow side-channels where unconscious degradation has made its inexpugnable home, and sits veiled with refuse. You pass above lines of railway, which cleave the region with black-breathing fissures. You see the pavements half occupied with the paltriest and most sordid wares; the sign of the pawnbroker is on

every hand; the public-houses look and reek more intolerably than in other places. The population is dense, the poverty is undisguised. All this northward-bearing tract, between Camden Town on the one hand and Islington on the other, is the valley of the shadow of the vilest servitude. Its public monument is a cyclopean prison; save for the desert ground around the Great Northern Goods Depot, its only open ground is a malodorous cattle-market. In comparison, Lambeth is picturesque and venerable, St. Giles is romantic, Hoxton is clean and suggestive of domesticity, Whitechapel is full of poetry, Limehouse is sweet with sea-breathings.

This is only a species of aside in a tale of the slums; to find Gissing at his stylistic best, one reads *Ryecroft* or the books on Dickens, work that came easily to him. Yet it is not in description or narration that his chief talent lay, but in the gradual revelation of the minds and hearts of his characters. He is not fertile in his invention of men and women—and, indeed, while he has a powerful intellect, he has small creative imagination. His best depictions are of a few types of humanity reproduced with variations in most of his novels: the young man in solitude (Waymark in *The Unclassed*, Peak in *Born in Exile*); the woman fiercely weak (Emma in *A Lodger in Maze Pond*;[2] Carrie in *Workers in the Dawn*); the grim old man (Alfred Yule in *New Grub Street*, Lord in *In the Year of Jubilee*); the unworldly lover of books (Christopherson in the story of that name;[3] Grail in *Thyrza*); and a dozen others, each of which, perhaps, had his prototype in Gissing's personal history. The girl of noble sincerity, the intellectual charlatan, the domineering woman of position, the discontented working-man, the predestined spinster, the meditative clergyman, the naïve reformer—these nearly complete his roster. The better ones stick in your memory. Deliberately abandoning the depiction of eccentricity (which Dickens so loved) because Gissing believed eccentricity to be dying under modern standardization, confining himself to common enough scenes and incidents, he succeeds all the same in putting living beings into our imagination. An attentive reader of *New Grub Street* probably will retain a permanent impression of five characters—Reardon, Biffen, Amy, Alfred Yule, Jasper Milvain. There are not many writers who can do as much with the images of substantially normal people.

What makes Gissing's power of fastening upon our memory more remarkable, is that it is accomplished without true plot. In the novels

[2] A short story reprinted in *The House of Cobwebs*. (P. C. 1967.)
[3] *Ibid*. (P. C. 1967.)

he wrote at the height of his abilities, very little happens—little, that is, which the reader was not sure would happen after he had got through the second chapter. Violence is rare, there is no exaggeration of the picturesque, events move relentlessly toward that baffling of hopes which we know from the first to be inevitable. Much of the ruddy colour of Morrison's stories of the East End is avoided deliberately. What Gissing does, he achieves by the power of the word and the appeal to universal experience. The half-chapter which describes the interview at a coffee-stand between sour old Alfred Yule and the beggar, once a surgeon, who tells him that he is doomed to blindness—this is perhaps the best instance, in *New Grub Street* or elsewhere, of Gissing's faculty for transmuting the ingredients of realism into something unexcelled in its kind. The conversation is done; Yule gives the pauper a five-shilling fee and walks home; it is the end for the two of them. This grim restraint, this 'minor key' as Gissing calls it, requires a disciplined style. Style Gissing has.

IV

A tormented soul, a pessimistic view, a memorable style—these only would not suffice to keep the grass green on Gissing's grave. But conjoined to them is the fact that Gissing was a moralist. His literary course was a search for moral purpose. If the aim of literature be to prove that there is purpose in nothing, it follows that there can be little purpose in books. Such a dilemma most pessimistic realists confront; but Gissing escapes by his belief in a Good. It is not the good of Christianity, nor yet the good of the materialistic reformer, but a pagan good—the good of Epicurus. Gissing refers only once to that philosopher, and then in a diary-entry remarking that a bust of Epicurus, in Rome, has a long nose. True Epicureanism permeated Gissing, all the same—the real Epicurean spirit of quiet resignation, retirement from ambition, the simple pleasure of contemplation, a gentleman's morality of peace and moderation, a pervading determination to live with dignity. It is easy to forget that Epicurus was a lofty moralist. But there were Right and Wrong for the Greek; and they were as real for Gissing. No divine justice rules Gissing's world; virtue has no certain desert, vice no sure penalty; but there lies behind Gissing's books the premise that one follows the good because it is beautiful and wise. This moral element won for Gissing in America the praise of Paul Elmer More and other humanists.

From half the hints one receives concerning Gissing, the reader approaching this realist for the first time might think him hardly a fit teacher of morals. Mutterings about 'morbid theories of sex', ominous phrases concerning a wasted life, rest in actuality upon only two little dark spots in a career of hardship. When young and enthusiastic, Gissing filched some coins to assist a girl of the streets, and paid for it with a prison sentence; and when a lonely man nearing his end, he committed adultery by going off to France with a woman not his wife—an offence much mitigated, perhaps, by the fact that Edith Gissing had for years been in a madhouse.[4] Otherwise, his was a remarkably conscientious life, full of diligence, affection, and fidelity to principle—a life not unworthy of some philosopher out of Diogenes Laertius.

In Gissing's books there is no assurance that virtue has its material reward; indeed, it often encounters disaster; but neither is there any suggestion that a man should live otherwise than honourably. Godwin Peak, tired of life that meant loneliness, ends miserably somewhere in Italy;[5] and Bruno Chilvers has a fashionable parish; but who would be Chilvers? Here is that brave defiance of adversity, that manliness, already remarked in Gissing. On the other hand, neither is roguery triumphant: Glazzard, his jealous revenge done, knows to what he has shrivelled in the process; Dyce Lashmar, the charlatan, disastrously overreaches himself. Ecclesiastes, from which Gissing liked to quote, was branded upon his heart.

To break with the modern world, to live as a man of gentle instincts and sound sense should, in such retirement as he can seek out—this is the only hope and consolation Gissing offers those who read him: this, and life lighted by truth. But then, Epicurus himself could do no more, and Epicurus left us no book like *Ryecroft*.

Life is done—and what matter? Whether it has been, in sum, painful or enjoyable, even now I cannot say—a fact which in itself should prevent me from taking the loss too seriously. What does it matter? Destiny with the hidden face decreed that I should come into being, play my little part, and pass again into silence; is it mine either to approve or to rebel? Let me be grateful that I have suffered no intolerable wrong, no terrible woe of flesh and spirit, such as others—alas! alas!—have found in their lot. Is it not much to have accomplished so large a part of the mortal journey with so much ease? If I find myself astonished at its

[4] She was confined to a lunatic asylum over four years *after* he left her. (P. C. 1967.)

[5] Actually in Vienna, but he came from Italy. (P. C. 1967.)

brevity and small significance, why, that is my own fault; the voices of those gone before had sufficiently warned me. Better to see the truth now, and accept it, than to fall into dread surprise on some day of weakness, and foolishly to cry against fate. I will be glad rather than sorry, and think of the thing no more.

Thus *The Private Papers of Henry Ryecroft*. 'I am inclined to think he died of congestion,' writes Norman Douglas, in *Siren Land*, 'for there was that within him—some macrocosmic utterance—which vainly endeavoured to pierce the gathering mists of introspection: the Ryecroft litany, beloved of weaker brethren, marks the parabola into the unfolding gloom. The old, old story: inefficient equipment, not of intellectuality but of outlook and attitude, and likewise of *bête humaine*; of that tough, cheerful attitude which, sanely regarded, is but sanity itself.'

The measure of justice in this judgment on Gissing, like so many other criticisms from men he influenced somehow against their will, needs review. But whatever his flaws, fifty years have not effaced him; he is current. And a man who knows George Gissing has come a good way toward knowing the spirit of our age.

2

*George Gissing, Humanist**

STANLEY ALDEN

THE casual reader of critical reviews must have been struck by the recurrence of the name of George Gissing, a novelist who, in the normal course of things, ought to have been long ago forgotten. That the name of a writer whose career began forty years ago should persist in the columns of the reviewers is enough to establish the assumption that its owner must have in his work something either unique or uniquely said; must have either intrinsic or historical value. In the case of Gissing, one can but infer from the constant use of his name in a single connection that present-day reviewers and critics regard him as the father of what may be vaguely termed 'English naturalism', as opposed to that older type of realism of which in their respective times Fielding and George Eliot are exemplars. It is significant that Gissing's name almost invariably appears linked with the names of three or four Continental novelists of his own or a slightly earlier day; with Dostoievsky, Zola, Balzac, and, less often, with Daudet. Seldom is he accounted brother to Howells or George Moore. And, in common with his more widely-known European contemporaries just mentioned, he is invariably—or all but invariably—dubbed 'naturalist', with the implication of praise. From such linkings it seems safe to infer that he is regarded as the same sort of naturalist, or realist (for the terms are loosely used), as his Continental confrères, while differing not only from his British contemporaries, but from the older English and American realists as well. What does such a distinction imply? Obviously that as it is habitually used, 'realism' means writing that deals with a certain type of matter; a type that may be roughly defined as that dealt with by Zola, or by Hardy in such a novel as *Jude the Obscure*. In other words, our younger critics have been using

* Reprinted from the *North American Review*, September 1922, pp. 364-77, by permission of the editors.

the words 'realist' and 'naturalist' almost interchangeably, and chiefly to characterize writers preoccupied with a particular *milieu*, rather than to identify a method of treatment, or an underlying purpose.

Into such a category it is possible to fit Gissing with no close familiarity with his works. For casual readers he is merely the author of such reprinted novels as *New Grub Street, The Whirlpool,* or possibly *The House of Cobwebs,* a volume of short stories which have had some vogue. If other titles are known, some of them suggest matter in the province of the naturalist. *The Unclassed,* for instance, or *The Nether World,* and *Human Odds and Ends* might carry such a suggestion. It will, therefore, be seen to be significant that he has not been mentioned along with Fielding and Eliot on the one hand, nor with George Moore or Howells on the other, for, with the exception of Mr. Moore, these writers have been distinguished as realists not so much by their subjects as by their literary methods and their philosophy. It is worth while to seek a reason why George Gissing has not long since been forgotten. Is it that as an innovator George Gissing has importance historically, or has he something to say which teases the interest of novel-readers, and may even trouble the complacency of critics who dispose of him so cavalierly with a word?

Mr. Frank Swinnerton in his critical study of Gissing makes it clear that he does not consider him a realist, but dismisses the matter summarily with the remark, 'He is too personal,' evidently disagreeing with Gissing himself when he says: 'But there can be drawn only a misleading, futile distinction between novels realistic and idealistic. It is merely a question of degree and of the author's temperament.' Thus Gissing plainly understood the word as applied to manner. Now an opinion on such a matter as realism from so distinguished a realist as Mr. Swinnerton is not to be lightly dismissed, but one regrets that he has not buttressed it with additional reasons, or taken occasion to 'place' Gissing with reference to his literary type. It may be valuable to consult with reference to the matter, others of his fellow-craftsmen.

Discussing 'Mr. George Gissing' in his volume *Fame and Fiction,* Mr. Arnold Bennett says: 'To take the common gray things which people know and despise and without tampering to disclose their epic significance, their grandeur—that is realism, as distinguished from idealism or romanticism.' (This comment about Gissing is best understood when one recalls that Mr. Bennett regards *The Nether*

World as his 'most characteristic novel'.) Here we see that realism includes both matter and manner with equal emphasis on each.

Mr. H. G. Wells, writing in *The Monthly Review*, remarks that 'he whose whole life was one unhappiness because he would not face realities, was declared the master and leader of the English realistic school'. If, then, Gissing's novels are what Leslie Stephen believes novels should be, 'transfigured experience—based upon direct observation and the genuine emotions which it has inspired', one could hardly expect them to be realistic, for Mr. Wells is right in asserting that he was afraid of facing, in his own life, the stern realities. His ineptitude in money-matters, a defect which he bestows so liberally upon his leading characters, is a case in point. Surely an anomaly this, a realist who shuns reality.

Gissing's own ideas on realism are illuminating. In his invaluable study *Charles Dickens*, for instance:

> In what degree, and in what direction, does he [Dickens] feel himself at liberty to disguise facts, to modify circumstances for the sake of giving pleasure or avoiding offence?
>
> Our 'realist' will hear of no such paltering with truth. Heedless of Pilate's question, he takes for granted that the truth can be got at, and that it is his plain duty to set it down without compromise; or, if less crude in his perceptions, he holds that truth, for the artist, is the impression produced on him, and that to convey this impression with entire sincerity is his sole reason for existing. To Dickens such a view of the artist never presented itself. Art, for him, was art precisely because it was not nature. Even our realists may recognize this, and may grant that it is the business of art to select, to dispose—under penalties if the result be falsification.

Here we see something of what realism meant to Gissing, as we do also when he refers to Balzac, Victor Hugo, Dostoievsky, and Daudet as 'Realists . . . men with an uncompromising method, and utterly heedless as to whether they give pleasure or pain'.

With distinguished insight he blames Dickens for fearing to write of disagreeable facts, so that he commits a capital artistic crime by causing Little Em'ly to seem to flee with Steerforth for mercenary reasons, while if the affair had been shown as Dostoievsky would have displayed it, with abundant though disagreeable detail, we should have been able to understand Emily's temptation, and to sympathize with her weakness. George Eliot, he points out, is, like Dickens, at fault in not motivating more fully the fall of Hetty, in *Adam Bede*. Out of deference for British susceptibility these two realists of an older school tampered with their 'fact' and thus falsified, artistically, in a way that would have been impossible to Gissing, or to the leading Continental realists. Again, he speaks of the difference between Dickens and the novelists of the French and the Russian schools, 'a difference which seems to involve the use of that very idle word "realism" '.

But by whatever type-name he would have chosen to call the novelist, Gissing's conception of him should be clear: 'truth, for the artist, is the impression produced on him' and his business is to convey that impression with 'entire sincerity'—a fine ideal, and one which Gissing attained in no mean degree. It is not by choice that he writes so largely of the submerged or semi-submerged world. He wrote most frequently of the people, the places, and the life that he knew best; the life of a literary toiler in London, a young man educated usually above his class and thus alien from it, as well as from the casual associates which his poverty and lack of social connections forced upon him. In a number of novels this hero recurs. Godwin Peak will come to the minds of those who have read that not very life-like novel, *Born in Exile*. And besides him there are Earwaker, Piers Otway, Osmond Waymark, Julian Casti, Kingcote, Harold Biffen, and Whelpdale, and other less conspicuous wanderers in 'the Valley of the Shadow of Books'. But he does not confine himself to portraying the unfortunate dwellers in the poorer quarters of London, though he is best known as the exponent of Lambeth, Clerkenwell, Tottenham Court Road, and of all that sordid East Side which, in so different a guise, is now being pictured by Mr. Thomas Burke.

The glimpses one gets in the Gissing novels of Surrey, Yorkshire, Devon and Cornwall, and the detailed pictures of Italy and Greece, are no less vivid and no less accurate and complete in detail. Of the life in these places, however, we hear less, and certainly what he tells us makes no such lasting impression as those pictures of squalor and distress with which his London scene abounds. Mr. A. C. Benson says of Gissing's novels that they had, 'when he treated of his own peculiar stratum, the same quality of hard reality which I value most of all in a work of fiction. The actors were not so much vulgar as underbred; their ambitions and tastes were often deplorable. But one felt that they were real people.' If we were speaking of Gissing's settings alone, realistic would be a fairly adequate tag; but obviously enough, setting is only the background for his picture of life.

In these settings one constantly happens upon bits of description so striking as to fix themselves in the consciousness like a vivid dream:

> An evil smell hung about the butchers' and the fish shops. A public-house poisoned a whole street with alcoholic fumes; from sewer-grates rose a miasma that caught the breath. People who bought butter from the little dealers had to carry it away in a saucer, covered with a piece of paper, which in a few minutes turned oily dark. Rotting fruit, flung out by costermongers, offered a dire regale to little ragamuffins prowling like the cats and dogs. Babies' bottles were choked with thick-curdling milk, and sweets melted in grimy little hands.

This, with its appeal to so many of our senses, is the sort of thing that earns him his title, realist. But it is not always of the disagreeable that he gives these pictures:

> An exquisite after-glow seemed as if it would never pass away. Above thin, grey clouds stretching along the horizon a purple flush melted insensibly into the dark blue of the zenith. Eastward the sky was piled with lurid rack, sullen-tinted folds edged with the hue of sulphur. The sea had a strange aspect, curved tracts of pale blue lying motionless upon a dark expanse rippled by the wind. Below me, as I leaned on the sea-wall, a fisherman's boat crept duskily along the rocks, a splash of oars soft-sounding in the stillness.

Such passages and others as carefully wrought are legitimately realistic, if by this term we mean that they have been written from actual observation and that they represent the impression made upon the author, reproduced without that 'tampering' which Mr. Arnold Bennett decries. Seldom indeed does one detect any tampering, any attempt to suppress evidence, to falsify logical conclusions for the sake of public taste. Especially in his earlier work is it observable that Gissing permits a flat and uninteresting ending, strongly suggestive of the Russians, rather than by an artificial heightening, an ending of the sort nine-tenths of all English and American fiction has led us to expect, and which even so veracious a writer as Dickens (as Gissing points out) was almost always guilty of. The endings of *The Nether World, The Emancipated, Thyrza, A Life's Morning,* and of most of his short stories, will illustrate the point. In no case, even where there is comparative happiness at the end, does the outcome seem other than the logical one, or the story fail of being a faithful presentation of life.

Now Mr. Swinnerton, very properly, is thinking of the substance of Gissing's novels when he says that he is 'too personal' to be a realist. Does he mean by this remark any more than that he has too often used himself, in one guise or another, for hero, and that because he represents his own special angle of vision he falls short of that impossible objectivity which so many present-day realists claim for themselves? Mr. Swinnerton is in agreement with Mr. Thomas Seccombe as to Gissing's being 'too personal', for the latter in his introduction to *The House of Cobwebs,* beyond question the most valuable because the most sympathetic study of Gissing (and one to which Mr. Swinnerton acknowledges indebtedness), says:

> He has no objectivity. His point of view is almost entirely personal. It is not the *lacrimae rerum*, but the *lacrimae dierum suorum*, that makes his pages often so forlorn. His laments are all uttered by the waters of Babylon in a strange land. His nostalgia in the land of exile, estranged from every refinement, was greatly enhanced by the fact that he could not get on with ordinary men, but exhibited almost to the last a practical incapacity, a curious inability to do the sane and the secure thing.

A little earlier in the same article Mr. Seccombe says of his realism:

> His approximation at times to the confines of French realistic art is of the most accidental and incidental kind.

And he continues by saying that he is 'a thorough moralist and sentimentalist'. Sentimentalist he may have been, if by the expression one means that he drew an occasionally sentimental picture of a young woman, but in the deeper implications of the word, he was far from sentimental. That is, emotion for its own sake he constantly decried, and it is in the more intellectually sympathetic relations of women and men that he finds their truest self-expression. When Alma Rolfe consents to being reasonable and trying to understand the point of view of her husband, she is most lovable and winning, and Nancy Tarrant dons her aureole only when she is sweetly reasonable. His women who have risen above merely sentimental relationships with men are those whom he most lovingly delineates: Ida Starr, Irene Derwent, Thyrza, Rhoda Nunn, and Miriam Baske, after she has become Mrs. Ross Mallard. He would have said of his realism that 'it is merely a question of degree and of the author's temperament'.

Although his attitude toward women is often slightly contemptuous, a circumstance not difficult to understand when one considers his marital tragedies, he seems to have had a deep and almost mystical reverence for womanhood. Apart from his more or less distorted and grotesque pictures of womankind, one recalls his many idealized portraits of girls. To mention some of the more conspicuous, there are: Cecily Doran, a lovely and vivid maiden, dimming slightly into a too-self-immolating wife; Sidwell Warricombe, conventional but of a quiet and virginal charm; Irene Derwent; Thyrza, a greatly idealized character in the book to which she gives her name, one of his most delicately wrought novels; Adela Waltham; Jane Snowdon, touching bit of humanity tossed up by the wave of slum-life in London; and the too ethereal Veranilda.

There is moreover a vein of the romantic in his preoccupation with little-known places. His characters have a way of going off suddenly to Odessa, St. Jean de Luz, Honolulu, Tasmania or the Bahamas, and their mastery of foreign languages and familiarity with out-of-the-way literature is astounding. Someone has always returned from a trip round the world, or is setting forth for Egypt or Queensland. All his chief characters are citizens of the world and by preference of that part of the world distant from main-travelled roads.

Besides these evidences, one may point to his humanitarian and romantic interest in animals and in the suppression of war. Marcella Moxey is (ironically enough) killed by the kick of a horse that she is defending from his cruel driver; in *The Crown of Life* there is bitter satire on the wanton shooting of wild birds, and Lee Hannaford, the inventor of highly destructive munitions, is mercilessly flayed. But I do not mean to show that these romantic and idealistic interests predominate; only to show that 'it is merely a question of degree', and that to dub Gissing 'realist', unqualifiedly, is not warrantable, any more than it would be to call him 'romanticist' or 'idealist'. Some larger category is needed, one taking into account not only his literary methods and temperamental leanings but also his central philosophy, for this is one of his chief merits and raises him above the level of the minor novelists who were his contemporaries—above his brother Algernon, for instance—as well as above most of his successors.

In discussing Gissing's philosophy one must remember that he lived chiefly by his pen, or by the equally exhausting business of private teaching. This fact, and the one that his formal education ended when he was a mere youth, are eloquent and account measurably for the crudity both in construction and content that all but the blindest of his critics must recognize in his books. A philosophy is the result of extensive and mature study as well as of having lived. The fact that as a boy of fifteen he won a first place in the kingdom in the Oxford local examinations says much for the calibre of his mind; a mind which if it had had the opportunity and leisure to flower would have been more orderly and better balanced. But his career at Owens College was sharply terminated through his boyish folly, and never again had he either the leisure or the opportunity for that rounded and traditional education which has done so much to produce the English gentleman and scholar.

Like his own Edwin Reardon in *New Grub Street*, he had ideals which, though they might repel the public, should have won for him a higher place than he now occupies. For he had ideas; a fact quite generally overlooked. At a time when all Europe was holding itself in leash while preparing for war, Gissing busied himself with exposing the futility of war; in *The Whirlpool* he discusses with much point the education of children; the inroads of manufacture upon village life and the impracticability of a communistic solution of the problem of labour and capital, he treats seriously in *Demos*, while he glances at it in *Ryecroft* and in some of his short stories such as *The Firebrand*;[1] scarcely one of his novels but contains a serious study of marriage. Note the following wise observation as to commerce:

> If trade is not to put an end to human progress, it must be pursued in Montcharmont's spirit. It's only returning to a better time; our own man of business is a creation of our own century, and as bad a thing as it has produced. Commerce must be humanized once more. We invented machinery, and it has enslaved us—a rule of iron, the servile belief that money-making is an end in itself, to be attained by hard selfishness.

Newspapers and periodicals, particularly those that cater to the ignorance and prejudices of their readers, he often satirizes, as for instance when he has Whelpdale hit upon the expedient of changing the name of his journal *Chat* to *Chit-Chat*, and of reducing the length of the articles to correspond to the average reader's capacity for sustained attention. Only now, in America, are we beginning to observe the deleterious effect of cheap journalism (aided unfortunately just now by the more pernicious moving-picture) upon the power to sustain attention. We have discovered a system for de-intellectualizing the drama, the novel, and even the essay.

[1] Reprinted in *Human Odds and Ends* and *Short Stories of To-day and Yesterday*. (P. C. 1967.)

At a time when few novelists in England spoke with understanding of the new place that woman is destined soon to fill, he constantly pointed to the necessity for widening her horizons by humane education. The following is from *Born in Exile* (1892):

The defect of the female mind? It is my belief that this is nothing more nor less than the defect of the uneducated human mind. I believe most men among the brutally ignorant exhibit the very faults which are cried out upon as exclusively feminine. A woman has hitherto been an ignorant human being; that explains everything.

Although this sounds somewhat old-fashioned hardly a generation after it was written, one recognizes that by no means all of the novel-reading world has even yet come to understand its underlying truth.

But while making these discriminating observations he recognizes the evil results sure to come from imperfect and nominal education of women—or of such education in general—which he exposes to ridicule in *In The Year of Jubilee*, particularly through Jessica Morgan, with her dry manuals and little black-bound note-books wherein she marshals her dates and facts against the coming examinations. Nancy and Horace Lord, and Samuel Barmby, in the same novel, are also shown to be the victims of this charlatan-education. Gissing's England was suffering from the malady of a newly-popularized education, with its wide but superficial appeal, in a way similar to that in which the United States is suffering today.

It seems to me as I read Gissing chronologically, that he made progress through the twenty-three years of his literary career, not always in artistry, but certainly in philosophical grasp of the implications of life, until at the end he had come firmly to believe that man is indeed the measure of all things. Beginning with the larger social problems of the mid-century, problems with which his idol Dickens, Kingsley, Ruskin, and Carlyle were likewise deeply concerned, he gradually worked away from these, since he found them insoluble (and because he found them so, earned in company with all humanists, the mob-bestowed title of 'pessimist'), to the basic problem of man's nature and its betterment. Here he is more nearly in the tradition of Meredith, Browning, and Matthew Arnold.

Yes, on the whole, Gissing is on the side of the humanistic angels. But he did not immediately nor easily take his place there, partly because of those very defects in education which he exposes in some of his characters, and partly because of the devastating poverty that prevented normal contact with human life and its sanative power.

A world of evidence for his humanism could be adduced, but let me present all that seems needful, under his conception of the gentleman; his recognition of the importance of the individual as embodying, in little, the human race; and his emphasis upon what is characteristic, as the essential thing.

Fortunately in his *Charles Dickens* he has given us his notion of a gentleman, a valuable contribution to the study of any writer's philosophy:

I cannot fall in with the common judgment that Dickens never shows a gentleman. Twice, certainly, he has done so, with the interesting distinction that in one case he depicts a gentleman of the old school; in the other, a representative of the fine manhood which came into existence (or became commonly observable) in his latter years. In John Jarndyce I can detect no vulgarity; he appears to me compact of good sense, honour, and gentle feelings. His eccentricity does not pass bounds; the better we know him the less observable it grows.

In other words, Gissing recognizes that there is a standard or normal gentleman by whom we may measure any pretender to that grand old title. Sir Leicester Dedlock he finds not quite a gentleman because 'his special characteristics overcharge the portrait'. He is too far from the typical or normal. He calls Cousin Feenix (in *Dombey and Son*) one of Dickens's best sketches of an aristocrat because 'his heart is right, his apprehensions are delicate'.

One of his most widely quoted and soundest dicta is on just this point of refinement of the feelings: it is from *The Private Papers*, and he is speaking of his housekeeper.

In my youth, looking at this man and that, I marvelled that humanity had made so little progress. Now, looking at men in the multitude, I marvel that they have advanced so far.

Foolishly arrogant as I was, I used to judge the worth of a person by his intellectual power and attainment. I could see no good where there was no logic, no charm where there was no learning. Now I think that one has to distinguish between two forms of intelligence, that of the brain, and that of the heart, and I have come to regard the second as by far the more important. I guard myself against saying that intelligence does not matter; the fool is ever as obnoxious as he is wearisome. But assuredly the best people I have known were saved from folly not by the intellect but by the heart. They come before me, and I see them greatly ignorant, strongly prejudiced, capable of absurd mis-reasoning; yet their faces shine with the supreme virtues, kindness, sweetness, modesty, generosity. Possessing these qualities, they at the same time understand how to use them; they have the intelligence of the heart.

Perhaps Gissing's own gentlemen may seem a trifle anaemic, bookmen, self-centred and aloof, yet he has created some rather vigorous types who would not measure so badly by the standard gentleman. For examples, there are: Ross Mallard, especially after he has been humanized by marriage; Hugh Carnaby, surely vigorous enough; Edmund Langley; and, of course, Ryecroft himself.

In *Born in Exile* he once bursts forth: 'I can't pretend to care for anything but individuals.' Later, in *Our Friend the Charlatan*, Sir William Amys, one of the few sound characters in this melodramatic and mechanical picture of types the author hated, remarks:

> I don't know that I have much faith in leagues. I am a lost individualist. Let everyone try to civilize himself; depend upon it, it's the best work he can do for the world at large.

Now although Gissing's preoccupation is with the individual, especially in his later work, he sees that the individual is valuable only as he is limited by human law: as a member of society. 'Never yet did true rebel, who has burst the barrier of social limitations, find aught but *ennui* in the trim gardens beyond', he says in *The Nether World* (1889), at a time when he was groping for and just beginning to discover the significance of life. The English novelist would have been in complete accord with the Norwegian diplomatist and scholar, Mr. Sigurd Ibsen, when he says:

> I cannot discover any thoughtlessness, any defective power of judgment, in the appreciation of the great personality in itself, without regard to the service he has done or the harm he has caused. On the contrary: I see in this a sound and correct judgment, which feels that the greatest values must be sought in the human being as such, and that they who in their own existences have shown us a human summit, have rendered the most excellent service possible to perform.

Gissing's appreciation of the importance of the characteristic, as opposed to the merely accidental or individual, is no less real than his grasp of the theory that the business of mankind is to produce as its crowning achievement the perfect human being. Sigurd Ibsen once more may be his spokesman:

> As a rule, it is in what is characteristic that we find what is worthy. The superiority of a rose in our eyes, consists in those qualities that distinguish it from other flowers, and the horticulturist's efforts are not directed towards obliterating these qualities by driving them back to

common type, but, on the contrary, to force them more to the foreground so that the rose becomes even more a rose than it was before. Likewise should the task of culture be to make man more and more manlike.

In discussing Dickens's character-drawing, Gissing praises Mrs. Gamp as a singular example of excellence of her kind. After saying that she represents the most delicate idealism, he calls this picture 'a sublimation of the essence of Gamp', and continues:

> No novelist (say what he will) ever gave us a picture of life which was not idealized; but there are degrees, degrees of purpose and of power. Juliet's nurse is an idealized portrait, but it comes much nearer to the real thing than Mrs. Gamp; in our middle-class England we cannot altogether away with the free-spoken dame of Verona; we Bowdlerize her—of course damaging her in the process.

This passage throws light obliquely on Gissing's view of life at the same time that it shows his conception of the novelist's art: what is essential is the significant, the invaluable; and to exhibit this in art one must 'idealize', select—no transcript of life will suffice.

Are we not able, then, to unify his reading of life and of art, and to find in these, together, the quintessence of George Gissing? Realist he is only in part, and by no means in the commonly accepted sense of the word, for always, but especially toward the end of his career, he designed his books to body forth an interpretation of life, which interpretation is that the perfected individual (the man who keeps to a golden mean between the extremes of freedom and restraint), and not the mass, is mankind's chief concern. Never is he 'naturalist', for his philosophical emphasis of the distinction between nature as represented by civilized man and by 'outer nature' is an outstanding characteristic and separates him forever from those who for their gloss upon human nature study the barnyard fowls. In *Sleeping Fires* he has Langley say to Louis Reed: 'The world never had such need of the Greeks as in our time. Vigour, sanity, and joy—that's their gospel.' And it is Gissing's own gospel.

It has already been observed that at the outset of his career he was concerned with the problems of class, particularly with the lower middle class, and with those who having once belonged to it had through economic pressure sunk beneath and become a part of the flotsam of London. In those early novels he would study the conditions among these people, not very sympathetically to be sure, though I can by no means agree with anyone who holds that Gissing did not know them quite as well as anyone could who, not of them, was obliged to dwell among them. Strictly speaking, this class never has a spokesman, for it is and always will be inarticulate.

Toward the end of his life Gissing busies himself with the discovery of a working philosophy for the individual. Nowhere more than in *The Private Papers of Henry Ryecroft* and in *The Whirlpool* do we find his explicit answer to the question, 'What is the end of man?' Both Harvey Rolfe and Henry Ryecroft, I take it, stand forth his spokesmen. (It is hardly necessary now, to point out that *Ryecroft* is in no literal sense an autobiography, but it may be worth while to remark that it is much more truly biographical than that thinly masked malice and scandal, *The Private Life of Henry Maitland.*) Each of these two men finds himself absorbed in the solution of his relation to the universe, and each arrives at the conclusion that to make one's self the centre, to work for intensive not extensive development, is the thing to be desired. Rolfe would write the history of some corner of English soil (perhaps of a single market-cross), study the microcosm in order to understand the macrocosm. He is another less distinguished Henry Adams, only his twelfth century is a moment of time in the late nineteenth century, and his Chartres, some bit of ground 'that is forever England'. Ryecroft would spend his declining years amid the slopes of his beloved Devon, beguiled by the reading of old books and cheered by country rambles. Nature to Gissing was ever a solace, a guide, too, in that it spoke of the simple fundamental processes of living and growth, such as a man of his complex and not quite normal nature was likely to forget. One would like to think of this tired, ill and unhappy writer, the scholar *manqué*, the misunderstood and little-appreciated philosopher, as having opened his eyes for the last time upon the sweet Devon meadows instead of the unfriendly mountains in alien St. Jean de Luz.[1]

[1] Actually, Gissing died at Ispoure, near St. Jean-Pied-de-Port. He was buried at St. Jean-de-Luz. (P. C. 1967.)

3

*Gissing as a Portrayer of Society**

RUTH CAPERS MCKAY

THE last twenty-five years of the nineteenth century were restless with a dozen theories of new thought, new science and new religion. All the accepted doctrines of Christianity, democracy and art, by which previously the Englishman had been content to mould his life and his philosophy, were shaken to their depths by impudent and fearless doubt. Huxley and Harrison struck at the orthodox theology of the Church of England. Carlyle and Arnold expressed a strong distrust of the workings of democracy. Ruskin with the practical aid of William Morris strove to inculcate new theories of art based on original observation rather than ancient prejudice. Arnold and Ruskin with pedantic assurance attempted to teach the average citizen plus his commonplace family how to fly to the heights of culture. It was an age of the spreading of wings—for the individual, education; for the nation, imperialism.

George Gissing was keenly aware of the activities of his age. In his novels we find frequent references to the life of that period, the new interest in education, the new theories of art, the changes in living conditions, the unions, the wars and rumours of wars, the current philosophies, the coming writers, the plays just produced, the popular lecturers, the fashions in music. Furthermore his letters to his family bear constant reference to and comment upon passing events. It is quite evident that he read newspapers as well as books. This interest in people, resulting in keen observation and reflection on Gissing's part, made his characterizations the most powerful feature of his ability as a novelist. The socialist and the philosopher in reading Gissing's novels may find in his characterizations alone the social and philosophic thought of a lifetime—the thought, in-

* Reprinted from Ruth Capers McKay, *George Gissing and his Critic Frank Swinnerton*, 1933, pp. 52-67, by permission of the University Press, Philadelphia.

cidentally, of a remarkably brilliant mind whose individuality of viewpoint gave an artistic piquancy to the tiresome details of life.

Although we cannot with any degree of certainty define limits to Gissing's faculty of observation (for in his letters to his family he frequently showed himself to be a gentle, home-loving man with a delightful sense of humour—in all, quite a contrast to the vehement novelist), yet we know that his power of artistic presentation took only certain forms. In portraying the very poor, such as are found in *The Nether World, Demos* and *Thyrza,* he was capable of viewing them only in the light of tragedy. This tragic point of view had two aspects which he used in alternating phases—the ironic and the pathetic. In any novel written of sad and unattractive circumstances, the effect is very depressing unless the tragedy is alleviated either by some comedy or by the inclusion of some incidents in the vein of 'looking on the bright side of life'—a sort of sentimental sop to ease the way. Gissing's humour was completely ironic and therefore its leavening qualities were very slight. The brightening incidents he conscientiously avoided as inartistic. Swinnerton, in one of his most successful and noteworthy books, *Young Felix*, has someone ask concerning his principal character, 'How is Felix? Still triumphing from failure to failure?' This short remark is symbolic of the attitude of the book—a toying with the balance of the elements of life—an easiness of viewpoint of which Gissing was never capable. To Gissing tragedy was tragedy and there was no sense in playing with it and making it appear as comedy. Other writers might do that because they wanted to please their readers (or for the better purpose of expressing an innate optimism), but Gissing cared nothing about pleasing his readers so he wrote under only two masters, art and truth. Add to these dominant forces his lack of optimism, and the so-called 'dreary quality' of his work is explained. Nearly all writers in describing the Crystal Palace on a Bank Holiday would have made it a highly amusing and delightful scene, which exuded satisfaction with life, and was a crowning tribute to the general good nature of the English people, holiday bent. But would not this very presentation show a lack of sympathy and understanding on the part of the author? This is merely a question for the purpose of piercing the indifference of the reader who says, 'Oh Gissing—he's so depressing, I can't read him'. And then turns to dear Dickens 'Because he pictures life so wonderfully'. But the person who does not care for Gissing is not apt to see the deep tragedy of Dickens—for underneath his pleasing style, Dickens was as much a tragedian as Gissing. However, some may feel that there was more skill in Dickens, because he was able to make unpalatable truths palatable.

Gissing, let me repeat, wrote of the tragedy of the very poor in two aspects, the pathetic, and the ironic—however, in the use of both he displayed remarkable powers of artistic presentation—he was a master of irony and of pathos. In dealing with the story in *Demos* of Mrs. Mutimer, who could not adjust herself to the rising fortunes of her family, and who with two servants or more in the house was only happy when she could sneak out into the kitchen and scour a pan or two, Gissing portrayed all the pathetic tragedy of the unchangeableness of caste. Mrs. Mutimer was a working man's wife, used to spending her life-energy in cleaning, washing, cooking, and managing her unruly family. When she was moved to a new house and her children expected her to sit all day in the parlour in a silk dress, her entire purpose in life was taken from her. Music, art, books, the theatre, had never featured in her existence—she could not turn to them now. Her tragedy consisted in that very change which most people would have considered a great stroke of good fortune. The pathos in men's lives was always apparent to Gissing—the danger lay in the fact that the continual striking of one chord of feeling lessened its effectiveness.

Gissing's irony developed many shadings—all the way from the lightly humorous to the coldly contemptuous. An example of the former is found in this short passage in *The Nether World.*

> In the social classification of the nether world—a subject which so eminently adapts itself to the sportive and gracefully picturesque mode of treatment—it will be convenient to distinguish broadly, and with reference to males alone, the two great sections of those who do, and those who do not, wear collars. Each of these orders would, it is obvious, offer much scope to an analyst delighting in subtle gradation.

Then there is the irony which has in it the quality of pathos—a blending of aspects—which is illustrated by another passage from the same book.

> An hour later noises of a familiar kind sounded beneath the window. A woman's voice was raised in the fury of mad drunkenness, and a man answered her with threats and blows. 'That's Mother,' sobbed Pennyloaf. 'I knew she wouldn't get over today. She never did get over a Bank-holiday.'

> Mrs. Candy had taken the pledge when her husband consented to return and live with her. Unfortunately she did not at the same time transfer herself to a country where there are no beer-shops and no Bank-holidays. Short of such decisive change, what hope for her?

And finally there is the coldly contemptuous irony—more forceful but less subtle in effect. This particular passage is from *The Town Traveller*.

> There on the narrow seats with high wooden backs, as uncomfortable a sitting as could be desired, with food before him of worse quality and worse cooked than any but English-speaking mortals would endure, he always felt at home, and was pleasantly reminded of the days of his youth, when a supper of eggs and bacon at some such resort rewarded him for a long week's toil and pinching. Sweet to him were the rancid odours; delightfully familiar the dirty knives, the twisted forks, the battered teaspoons; not unwelcome the day's newspaper splashed with brown stains of coffee and spots of grease. He often lamented that this kind of establishment was growing rare, passing away with so many other features of old London.

In the portrayal of the poor, Gissing was certainly the 'mouth-piece of misery'—he made demands upon the sympathy and understanding of his reader which the average person was unable to meet. Those who peruse his stories of the trials and restrictions of poverty must not expect 'a pleasant hour's reading'—but rather a highly artistic elucidation of the less attractive features of this widely varying life. Gissing's novels will become popular in proportion to the increasing education of the reading public—as more and more we look to the novel for art rather than for amusement.

It is a singular fact that many find Gissing's portrayals of the middle class even more disturbing than those which picture people in the throes of dire poverty. The reason for this is that in poverty there are two limitations, lack of means and cultivation; but the middle class on the whole have only one limitation, that of the mind—the whole world of thought lies within their reach, have they but the power to grasp it. An ironic exposition of the mental limitation of the average man of the lower middle class is repulsive to the general public. It recoils in self-defence. And yet we all know that the limitation of the mind is a deeper and more irrevocable tragedy than the limitation of the purse.

Gissing's characters of the middle class may be divided into two groups, those who were intellectual and those who were not. The latter were by far in the majority; in fact, Gissing generally has a hero who shows a spiritual resemblance to the author and perhaps a heroine of unusual qualities of mind and the remainder are people of ordinary kin. I do not mean to suggest by this classification that the characters within the divisions lack variety; they are as diverse as life itself. Neither do the people termed 'mediocre' lack interest—it is the very simplicity of their minds which intrigues the reader's attention. Because of the Victorian method in which Gissing wrote, few novels of his can be said to be restricted to one class of society but there are some whose principal concern lies with the members of the middle class. A loose grouping of these would include *The Emancipated, New Grub Street, Born in Exile, Denzil Quarrier, The Odd Women, In the Year of Jubilee, The Paying Guest, Eve's Ransom, The Whirlpool, The Crown of Life, Our Friend the Charlatan,* and *Will Warburton. Isabel Clarendon* and *A Life's Morning*, showing the influence of the society novel, deal with a life above that of the middle class but not with the actual aristocracy. Gissing never came in contact with any Lords or Ladies and so fortunately he did not choose to portray them. As Swinnerton has intimated his characterizations in the upper classes were mostly those of people who had but recently left an inferior circle—not those who were 'to the manner born'.[1]

As has been suggested there is in each of Gissing's novels—with but few exceptions—a certain small group of people to whom he is temperamentally akin—those who have certain qualities of intellect similar to his own. Among the men outstanding examples are the vigorous thinker Osmond Waymark (*The Unclassed*), the nervously incapable Bernard Kingcote (*Isabel Clarendon*), the strongly individual Ross Mallard (*The Emancipated*), the frustrate Reardon, the poverty-stricken but valiant Biffen, the ingenuous Whelpdale (all in *New Grub Street*), the sensitive but aspiring Godwin Peak (*Born in Exile*), the visionary Langley (*Sleeping Fires*), the morose Maurice Hilliard (*Eve's Ransom*) and the mature philosopher Harvey Rolfe (*The Whirlpool*). These men, Waymark, Kingcote, Mallard, Reardon, Biffen, Whelpdale, Peak, Langley, Hilliard and Rolfe, have each a strong and distinctly individual personality; as a whole, however, they may be classed as the Gissing type because of their

[1] Lady Ogram (*Our Friend the Charlatan*), Lady Revill (*Sleeping Fires*) and Lord Polperro (*The Town Traveller*) were all of inferior birth. In fact, Lord Winterset (*Isabel Clarendon*) is Gissing's only drawing of the real nobility that is both successful and convincing.

spiritual resemblance to their author. They are all thinkers—individualists with scholarly inclinations; most of them have the urge to write; none of them is successful in a worldly sense. For some reason which seems to be peculiar to their natures they are all unfortunate in love. Their matrimonial intentions are not based upon the desire for a home and children, a pleasant domestic life, but rather upon the strong need created by their unhappy temperaments for comforting companionship—someone to whom they can turn when they wish to put aside the haunting thought of self. Love is with them an inverted emotion, based on their own desire for further happiness. They are on the whole distinctly a modern type.

With these men of intelligence should be placed several portrayals of women who are superior to the average in character and in thought. As early as the writing of *The Unclassed* Gissing attained a characterization of singular strength in Ida Starr—she is vivid and highly emotional, a young woman who beset by every conceivable disadvantage finally wins her battle with life. Then we find in succession five romantic creations—women whom Gissing sought to endow with a lasting charm. First there is Isabel in *Isabel Clarendon*, the best portrayal of a woman of high society in all of his books—a lady, and one to whom the manner of life means much. In *Demos*, Gissing drew Adela Waltham, a mere girl compared to Isabel who when that novel (*Isabel Clarendon*) opens and the love affair begins is nearly forty—a daring thing! Adela was ruled by her mother and when she finally came into the sovereignty of her own person it was too late to save herself from disaster. She is symbolic of the fate of a rare and lovely nature which is encompassed and finally ruined by family intrigue 'for her good'. In *Thyrza* Gissing attempted great things[2]—

[2] In a letter to his sister at the time of the book's conception he wrote thus:

I am living at present in Lambeth, doing my best to get at the meaning of of that strange world, so remote from our civilization. My book is practically still to begin, but I believe it will be my best yet. I have the strangest people and scenes floating in my mind. Tomorrow, a Bank Holiday, I must spend in the street; there is always much matter to be picked up on such days.

Ah, but you will see the result. I have a book in my head which no one else can write, a book which will contain the very spirit of London working-class life. Little by little it has been growing; it will be a stronger and profounder book than *Demos*. . . . With me it is a constant aim to bring the present and the past near to each other, to remove the distance which seems to separate Hellas from Lambeth. It can be done, by grasping firmly enough the meanings of human nature. (*Letters of George Gissing to His Family,* pp. 182, 183, and 184).

here is the Dickens quality at its best; and here is the influence of Daudet in the drawing of a white flower against the darkness of the slums. Thyrza is a vision: in one of his letters Gissing said of her, 'Thyrza herself is one of the most beautiful dreams I ever had or shall have. I value the book really more than anything I have yet done.'[3] She is not a study—there is little attempt to explain or justify her; an unfortunate habit noted in connection with other characterizations and which was the direct result of Gissing's all-enveloping sincerity. In the end Thyrza had to die just as Juliet had to die. Emily Hood (*A Life's Morning*) is a compromise between the visionary idealism of Thyrza and the psychological realism of life. *A Life's Morning* is considerably weakened by the necessity of explaining Emily—the obvious reasons for her actions and decisions are not sufficient—there are reasons within reasons, wheels within wheels. And then the absurdly happy ending, dictated by the publishers, makes unfortunately of this book—which has in separate parts many brilliant features—a complete failure.

In the succeeding novels as Gissing's power and aptitude developed we are amazed at the remarkable collection of women whom he presents. The men are interesting, excellent in many respects, but the women are remarkable! Who but Meredith has drawn a galaxy of portraits equally as fine! Even Swinnerton admits that here Gissing is master. In *The Emancipated* there is a portrait of a charming young woman, Cecily Doran, who has complete freedom of action—a rare thing for a woman of that period—and who is fired with all the current theories of intellectual emancipation. However, as captain of her fate she acts unwisely and marries offhand an amazing young philanderer, Reuben Elgar. Cecily bravely lives it out and becomes a more cautious woman but youth's fresh opportunity for happiness is lost to her forever.

Many of Gissing's women come into their happiness after the trial and disillusionment of a youthful choice. Isabel Clarendon had been miserably married before she met Kingcote and in the end she finds contentment as the wife of still another suitor. Adela Waltham (*Demos*) passes through her difficult marriage with Richard Mutimer and afterwards we are assured that she will find some peace in a second union with Hubert Eldon who, moreover, had been her first lover. Thyrza pledges herself to marry Gilbert Grail and then unfortunately meets Walter Egremont and conceives her tragic love for him. Emily Hood and Wilfrid Athel (*A Life's Morning*), a pair of

[3] *Letters of George Gissing to His Family*, p. 189.

romantic neurotics with whom it is difficult to sympathize, pass through an extraordinary amount of trouble and he even becomes engaged to another girl, the vivacious Beatrice Redwing, before their fate of perfect happiness together is achieved. In *The Nether World* Sidney Kirkwood and Jane Snowdon—obviously meant for each other if such things are written in an author's heaven—never become married. Amy Reardon (in *New Grub Street*) after her husband's death finds happy contentment as the wife of the more successful and practical Jasper Milvain—however, this leaves Marian Yule, the real heroine of the book and the former *fiancée* of Milvain, to eke out a frustrated life as her father's literary assistant.

In *Born in Exile*—to continue this series of troubled careers—Sidwell Warricombe lacks the courage necessary to cast her former life behind her and travel to Europe as Peak's wife. When the book closes she is still of the opinion that her choice, while unromantic, was wise. Lilian, the frail, ethereal mistress of Denzil Quarrier, has had a former unfortunate marriage which makes her legal union with Quarrier impossible and this serves as the foundation for the tragedy of the story. A series of catastrophes in *The Odd Women* continually defeats whatever well-meaning impulses the fates may have had. Even the love story of Rhoda Nunn and Everard Barfoot after some very hopeful scenes collapses when fulfilment is in sight. Rhoda expects too much and Barfoot is mere man—a reversal of the situation in *Eve's Ransom* when Hilliard expects too much and Eve is mere woman. The heroine of *In the Year of Jubilee*, Nancy Lord, has all kinds of remarkable difficulties before she finally emerges as the happy and contented wife of Lionel Tarrant, although, if one considers the characters of both, this seems an impossible achievement. *Eve's Ransom* has for its only plot the story of an unsuccessful love affair, and Eve, the centre of a conflagration, is in the midst of another affair when she meets Hilliard and at the conclusion is seen as the charming wife of still another man. Was romance ever so contrary? Finally in *The Whirlpool* Alma Frothingham—a creation to whom no critic has paid fitting tribute—takes a disillusioning continental trip before she agrees to marry Rolfe; and then later as a married woman attempts to continue the strategy which the continent had taught her. For every one of these women the course of true love, or in fact of any love, did not run smooth. Gissing when considering women seems of the conviction that love is very seldom transforming and that those natures who were restless, selfish, and dissatisfied before marriage are not apt to undergo a complete renaissance on the wedding day.

I was speaking of Cecily Doran (*The Emancipated*) when I was led astray by the diverse misfortunes of these attractive heroines. In the same book there is Miriam Baske, a devoutly religious young woman who has had rather an unsavoury past in a marriage made for money. Miriam finally finds herself—or perhaps she simply loses her former self—through the reading of Dante, and becomes so completely changed that in the end she is considered as a worthy mate for Ross Mallard. It is quite typical of Gissing that he should seek to explain the changes in Miriam's character as the result of her reading—he had absolute faith in the power of books. The transformation is not convincing because it is too complete. Mrs. Abbott, a minor character in *The Whirlpool*, also has a miraculous change of character so that the lady at the beginning and the lady at the end of the book hardly seem to be the same person. These were errors in Gissing's art—but they are minor and should be treated as such—small offences in the balance with his great achievements.

It would not be fair to omit from the study of Gissing's heroines those three most miserable sisters in *The Odd Women*. The eldest, Alice, is simply a dreary, well-meaning spinster and the youngest, Monica, a mere doll of a girl, but the second sister, Virginia, has a failing which places her, strange to say, among the best and most individual of Gissing's creations. It is only to Virginia in *The Odd Women* and Mrs. Mutimer in *Demos* that Swinnerton pays unalloyed tribute as character studies of faultless excellence. Virginia, as the reader soon becomes aware, is addicted to secret tippling; however, she covers it well and not until age and misfortune have weakened her reserve does her family discover the explanation of many little household mysteries. Virginia is a lady to whom the suggestion of the corner saloon was highly repulsive and so she is driven to practice with a canny furtiveness the last habit of which one would have suspected her. As Swinnerton says, 'Virginia Madden, when not quite herself, is great'.

I am inclined to think that in the restraint and artistic suggestiveness which Gissing showed in his drawing of the unforgettable Eve, we find the art which is the pure product of imaginative genius. Swinnerton has said, and justly, that in the writing of this book Gissing 'reached a point of detachment never attained elsewhere'. Eve is a delight and a mystery—delightful because of her elusive charm which is veiled in suggestiveness—mysterious because not once does the author allow us a glimpse of her mind, we know no more of her than does the bewitched Maurice Hilliard; and in the end he finds that he knew nothing. There is womanliness personified in Isabel Clarendon, the fresh graciousness of girlhood in Adela Waltham, the mystery of a spiritual beauty in Thyrza, the splendid strength of mind in Rhoda Nunn, all the treasures of refinement and culture which were Sidwell Warricombe's—but Eve, a mere working girl, superficially educated at best, lacking any of the advantages of family or a pleasant home background—Eve overshadows them all because she has some indefinable quality. One does not feel that Gissing created Eve but rather that she was a wistful shadow who passed with reluctance before his vision. He observed her as best he could, watching her as she moved quite without his control or by his design. She was never his creature, to twist and turn, to analyse with superior judgment. She was a mysterious, independent self.

When one considers that there are, to make a loose estimate, something more than three hundred important characters in Gissing's twenty-two novels, one realizes that there must have been included many people of ordinary life—just people—who play their parts, and not insignificant ones, in his books. Gissing was not an author who neglected details: if a character was to be included he was important enough to be the object of the writer's careful study. He had a gift for portraying family groups and the pleasant intricacies of their interrelationship. In Gissing's letters to his brothers and sisters he showed clearly how dear and real to him were the ties of family life. He was always inquiring about his mother, asking one sister as to the health of another, suggesting some change or some plan which they all might enjoy. Even in the midst of his own greatest trials his thought in his letters was first of them. As a result of this loving trait in his nature he drew in some of his novels delightful pictures of happy family life. In *Isabel Clarendon* the rector, Mr Vissian, his wife, and their fanciful little boy form a charming group with the shaded rectory, a venerable treasure house of books, as their centre of existence. The mutual affection which brightens the humble and meagre lives of Lydia and Thyrza Trent is as lovely a picture of sweetness and tenderness as Gissing ever drew. It is evidence of the novelist's fertile power that Lydia, in spite of the poetry and imaginative feeling which is showered on Thyrza, does not suffer in comparison but has an individuality of strength and of beauty which is all her own. In *Born in Exile* the Warricombes, father, mother, son and daughter, present as a whole the solid English family of the upper middle class; in the father and son may be found all of the breadth and equally all of the limitations of an Englishman of their class—unquestioning allegiance to the orthodox theology of the Church of England, a belief in honour which allows no merciful understanding to sway its dictates, and a strict sense of the dignity of self and of all that comprised self, particularly one's family. Sidwell as the daughter of the house was more pliable only because women are less vehement than men. The most perfect picture of English home life is that of the Mortons in *The Whirlpool.* It is amusing to note that Gissing includes even here his love of the classics.

The house had stood for a century and a half, and for eighty years had been inhabited by Mortons. Of its neighbours in the elm-bordered road, one or two were yet older; all had reached the age of mellowness. *'Sicut umbra praeterit dies'*—so ran the motto of the dial set between porch and eaves; to Harvey Rolfe the kindliest of all greetings, welcoming him to such tranquillity as he knew not how to find elsewhere. . . . His (Morton's) house was spacious, well-built, comfortable. The furniture, in great part, was the same his parents had used; solid mahogany, not so beautiful as furniture may be made, but serviceable, if need be, for another fifty years. He had a library of several thousand volumes, slowly and prudently collected, representing a liberal interest in all travail of the mind, and a special taste for the things of classical antiquity. Basil Morton was no scholar in the modern sense, but might well have been described by the old phrase which links scholar with gentleman. He lived by trade, but trade did not affect his life. The day's work over, he turned, with no feeling of incongruity, to a page of Thucydides, of Tacitus, or to those less familiar authors who lighted his favourite wanderings through the ruins of the Roman Empire.

In Mrs. Morton is pictured the ideal English mother:

Mrs. Morton had the beauty of perfect health, of health mental and physical. To describe her face as homely was to pay it the highest compliment, for its smile was the true life of the home, that never failed. *Filia generosi*, daughter of a house that bred gentlewomen, though its ability to dower them had declined in these latter days, she conceived her duty as wife and mother after the old fashion, and was so fortunate as to find no obstacle in circumstance. She rose early; she slept early; and her day was full of manifold activity. Four children she had borne—the eldest a boy now in his twelfth year, the youngest a baby girl; and it seemed to her no merit that in these little ones she saw the end and reason of her being.

If we turn to quite another stratum of society this illuminating passage in *Demos* stresses and explains Gissing's belief in the permanency of class distinction.

> It was the face of a man by birth and breeding altogether beneath her. Never had she understood that as now; never had she conceived so forcibly the reason which made him and her husband and wife only in name. Suppose that apparent sleep of his to be the sleep of death; he would pass from her consciousness like a shadow from a field, leaving no trace behind. Their life of union was a mockery, their married intimacy was an unnatural horror. He was not of her class, not of her world; only by violent wrenching of the laws of nature had they come together. She had spent years in trying to convince herself that there were not such distinctions, that only an unworthy prejudice parted class from class. One moment of true insight was worth more than all her theorizing on abstract principles. To be her equal this man must be born again, of other parents, in other conditions of life. 'I go back to London a mechanical engineer in search of employment.' They were the truest words he had ever uttered; they characterized him, classed him.

In all of Gissing's novels he clung to this theory of the fixity of class. This vision of an irrevocable fate may partly justify his continual use of the pathetic note in his portrayals of the poorer classes. It is in the same book (*Demos*) that he says, 'But we are interesting in proportion to our capacity for suffering, and dignity comes of misery nobly borne'. This statement of an artistic precept in which we may believe that the author had the utmost faith is very illuminating when one considers the type of novel which Gissing wrote—he was, on the whole, much more concerned with unhappiness than with happiness.

But it is a mistake to think that when Gissing leaves the poorer classes he loses his keen perceptive power. For instance, consider Mr. Musselwhite in *The Emancipated*: 'This gentleman suffered under a truly aristocratic affliction—the ever-reviving difficulty of passing his day.' Or again there is Madeline Denyer (*The Emancipated*) who as 'a creation in a paragraph' equals Jessica Morgan (*In the Year of Jubilee*).

> Madeline—whom her sisters addressed affectionately as 'Mad'—professed a wider intellectual scope; less given to the melting mood than Barbara, less naïve in her enthusiasms, she took for her province aesthetic criticism in its totality, and shone rather in censure than in laudation. French she read passably; German she had talked so much of studying that it was her belief she had acquired it; Greek and Latin were beyond

her scope, but from modern essayists who wrote in the flamboyant style she had gathered enough knowledge of these literatures to be able to discourse of them with a very fluent inaccuracy. With all schools of painting she was, of course, quite familiar; the great masters—vulgarly so known—interested her but moderately, and to praise them was, in her eyes, to incur a suspicion of philistinism. From her preceptors in this sphere, she had learnt certain names, old and new, which stood for more exquisite virtues, and the frequent mention of them with a happy vagueness made her conversation very impressive to the generality of people. The same in music. It goes without saying that Madeline was an indifferentist in politics and on social questions; at the introduction of such topics, she smiled.

In fact it is always in regard to women that Gissing has his clearest vision—again and again, he writes of them in words of such convincing truth that one wonders that even the austerity of his style has been able to keep him from acquiring that most lucrative of attainments, a feminine following. Mallard in *The Emancipated* is talking to his wife, the reclaimed Miriam, concerning Cecily whose husband has left her:

'Well, well; go and talk to the poor girl, and see if you can do anything. I wish she were an artist of whatever kind; then it wouldn't matter much. A woman who sings, or plays, or writes, or paints, can live a free life. But a woman who is nothing but a woman, what the deuce is to become of her in this position?'

What other English writer in 1890 was stating the truth concerning women with equal perception and clarity?

There are two types of men beside the intellectual which Gissing pictured with rare ability; one is the brusque outdoor British gentleman (those in this group Morley Roberts suggests are largely pictures of himself), and the other, the clever charlatan. The former may be found in its fullest development in the figure of Denzil Quarrier, a man who has all the obvious characteristics of healthy and temperate masculinity. Others of his kind are Alfred Waltham in *Demos*, Hugh Carnaby in *The Whirlpool*, Robert Narramore in *Eve's Ransom* (an admirable study, particularly in his subjection to Eve) and, but of a more crude variety, Mr. Gammon in *The Town Traveller*. They are kind at heart, apt to be indulgent regarding the weaker sex—with emphasis on the comparative connotation of the adjective—and in their playful moments are as ungainly as bears. Intuition with them is a purely feminine attribute. Humour takes the form of definite jokes. They are sometimes sportsmen, sometimes legislators, in either case the impulse being the desire for energetic action. They make good husbands, but in modern fiction they figure almost exclusively as 'the man who does not understand'.

In the drawing of the charlatan Gissing shows an unusual faculty, if we consider how far from his actual experience of life was any notion of shrewd business methods. There are grades of charlatanism of which the lowest is Dyce Lashmar (*Our Friend the Charlatan*), perfectly unscrupulous, clever, determined and an attractive and fluent talker. Equally hopeless is Daniel Otway, a rather jolly sinner in *The Crown of Life*, who goes his way with no thought of becoming penitent. A more serious conception is that of Eustace Glazzard in *Denzil Quarrier* whose story is given an unusually suggestive touch by his interest in modelling a head of Judas. Reuben Elgar (*The Emancipated*) and Vincent Lacour (*Isabel Clarendon*) are men whose clever faculties were exercised not with the idea of their advancement but with the sole intent of avoiding any type of work. For example, Lacour 'thought with contemptuous pity of the poor wretches who had to present themselves at bank, or office, or shop by a certain hour. "Under no circumstances whatever," he often said to himself with conviction, "would I support life in that way. If it comes to the worst, there are always the backwoods. Hard enough, no doubt, but that would be in the order of things." ' Lacour after several false starts manages to marry an heiress and so his happy fate is fulfilled. The most finished example of the charlatan type is however that of a man who blended with his charlatanism many good qualities—in fact, the reader is often in a quandary as to whether to applaud or condemn. Jasper Milvain in *New Grub Street* is the personification of shrewdness, displaying to a marked degree both its good and bad elements. But 'good and bad' are perhaps too definite, too strong in their connotations. There was nothing really 'bad' in Milvain—it was only that he sacrificed to the attainment of material success many of the things which are generally held highest. However, he almost managed to justify himself; he is fond of personal exposition.

But just understand the difference between a man like Reardon and a man like me. He is the old type of unpractical artist; I am the literary man of 1882. He won't make concessions, or rather, he can't make them; he can't supply the market. I—well, you may say that at present I do nothing; but that's a great mistake, I am learning my business. Literature nowadays is a trade. Putting aside men of genius, who may succeed by mere cosmic force, your successful man of letters is your skilful tradesman. He thinks first and foremost of the market; when one kind of goods begins to go off slackly, he is ready with something new and appetizing. He knows perfectly all the possible sources of income.

It is an interesting example of the technical care with which Gissing wrote all his novels, that in the early pages of *New Grub Street* when Milvain is first thinking of Marian, he remarks to his sisters, 'But it's a pity she doesn't play the piano'. After he has jilted Marian and married Amy Reardon, who through death and inheritance has become a rich widow, the novel closes with a clever scene between Milvain and his wife of which this is the concluding part.

'No, I am far from a bad fellow. I feel kindly to everyone who deserves it. I like to be generous, in word and deed. Trust me, there's many a man who would like to be generous, but is made despicably mean by necessity. . . . I have much of the weakness that might have become viciousness, but I am now far from the possibility of being vicious. . . . Happiness is the nurse of virtue. . . . Go to the piano, dear, and play me something. If I don't mind I shall fall into Whelpdale's vein, and talk about my "blessedness". Ha! Isn't the world a glorious place?'

'For rich people.'

'Yes, for rich people. How I pity the poor devils!—play anything. Better still if you will sing, my nightingale!'

So Amy first played, and then sang, and Jasper lay back in dreamy bliss.

So ends the story of Jasper Milvain—the heir to all New Grub Street.

It is hardly necessary to stress the exceptional manner in which these widely varying characters exemplified their age. There is the fallacy of the democratic theory as realized in Richard Mutimer (*Demos*); the radical philosophy of Osmond Waymark (*The Unclassed*); the problem of mental emancipation from the domestic point of view as seen by Cecily Doran (*The Emancipated*); the increase in education among women, pictured in its finest development in Rhoda Nunn (*The Odd Women*), in its worst, in Jessica Morgan (*In the Year of Jubilee*) and Madeline Denyer (*The Emancipated*); the new laxity in religious belief as Godwin Peak (*Born in Exile*) exemplified; the rising journalistic spirit in literature of which Jasper Milvain (*New Grub Street*) was a leader; the futility of social reform in the mistaken efforts of Walter Egremont (*Thyrza*); the blind individualism of Maurice Hilliard (*Eve's Ransom*); the contemptuous attitude towards patriotism and the ideals of this civilization as felt by Harvey Rolfe (*The Whirlpool*). Each character is a study of his age. If you desire to learn of the latter quarter of the nineteenth century and would have your knowledge of the spirit as well as the form, to read the novels of George Gissing is to reap a rich harvest.

4

*The Permanent Stranger**

'POOR Gissing,' said Henry James, recalling his sole meeting with his younger contemporary, 'struck me as quite particularly marked out for what is called in his and my profession an unhappy ending.' 'Poor Gissing': the adjective, attributive both of the most depressing poverty and of fecklessness in the affairs of life, has become conventional; and the novels of Gissing, one suspects, have been obscured by the legend of Gissing the man, the essence of which is contained in James's remark. And he himself helped to create the legend, not only in *New Grub Street* but more potently, perhaps, in his most popular book, *The Private Papers of Henry Ryecroft*, a work which certainly presents one aspect of the man but which is marred by complacency and a self-conscious superiority. 'A blend of autobiography, rumination, and the escape-dream,' Mr. Plomer calls it in his valuable introduction to this new edition of *A Life's Morning*, and of these elements it was the escape-dream which caught the public imagination. Gissing's wistful dream of himself as the scholar-recluse. But if he survives, it will be as a novelist alone, and a novelist of a distinct kind.

Whether because of the circumstances of his birth or, as is more likely, because of the defects in his character which caused him to break away from the course of life that could confidently have been predicted for him, Gissing became the first representative of a new type of novelist in English. Reading his work today one is immediately struck by its kinship in basic preoccupations with that of a later writer, D. H. Lawrence. Lawrence's fiction, it has recently been suggested, 'is mostly about class, not, as he supposed, about sex'. Similarly, Gissing's is mostly about class. Both came from the industrial north; both in their youth were 'great passers of examinations'; both were products of the new, provincial universities, which meant, however sound their education may have been, that they felt

* Reprinted from *The Times Literary Supplement*, February 14th, 1948, p. 92, by permission of *The Times*.

themselves at a disadvantage when compared with graduates of Oxford and Cambridge. Their origins, it is true, were markedly different; Lawrence's father was a miner, Gissing's a pharmaceutical chemist of some cultural and scientific attainment. But both found themselves, as a result of their talents and, in Gissing's case, as a result of an unfortunate marriage, outside their own class and ill at ease in any other; and both, though the reasons may have been different, shared an uncompromising hostility to the civilization in which they lived.

George Gissing was born in Wakefield on 22 November 1857. He was therefore almost exactly contemporary with George Moore, but unlike Moore, though he knew and admired the work of the great European novelists of his day, especially that of Turgenev, to whose review, *Le Messager de l'Europe*, he contributed a regular London letter, he was scarcely influenced by them. He remained faithful to the tradition of the Victorian three-volume novel and took over with it its apparatus of coincidence, eccentric wills, secret marriages and engagements, missing mothers and so on. In his best novels what he has to say is of such interest and is said so urgently that we scarcely heed the plots, but when his imagination is working at low pressure, as in *A Life's Morning*—a curious choice, one would have thought, for introducing modern readers to him—he writes in terms of pure Victorian melodrama. Yet he was a conscious artist. 'Human life,' he wrote to his brother in 1884, 'has little interest to me, on the whole—save as material for artistic presentation. I can get savage over social iniquities, but even then my rage at once takes the direction of planning revenge in artistic work'; and ten years later, he wrote in *Ryecroft*: 'It has occurred to me that one might define Art as: an expression, satisfying and abiding, of the zest of life.' The zest of life is not a quality we associate with Gissing, but his best, most enduring work is certainly the product of his peculiar relation to life. In the presence of life he appears to have had no defences at all; Wells notes, in his reminiscences of his friend in *An Experiment in Autobiography*, that 'he had no customary *persona* for miscellaneous use'. It was as though he had been flayed and must receive the buffetings of life on the naked nerves, which were exposed to all the manifestations of the age. So he was not in any sense a realist. He was a highly subjective writer, and his novels are cries of anguish and horror at the age as it had impressed itself upon him. It was Wells's view that 'he would not and perhaps could not look life squarely in the eyes', but this is not the impression we get from his novels today. Rather one would say that rarely have the especial qualities of any age been rendered with such passionate intensity. Exacerbated by what he had seen and suffered, protesting bitterly—'whimpering' is a word that has been used—he was aware all the time of the essential situation of his day with a sureness that few other English novelists have possessed. It was his misfortune, as far as material success was concerned, that his interpretation of the essential situation of the eighties was distasteful to his readers.

His first novel, *Workers in the Dawn*, published in 1880, was a propaganda novel. He soon outgrew his belief in socialism; in his second novel, *The Unclassed* (1884), he makes his hero Waymark, himself a novelist and, as the *Letters to Members of His Family* show, his spokesman, say:

> . . . I was not a conscious hypocrite in those days of violent radicalism, working-men's-club lecturing, and the like; the fault was that I understood myself as yet so imperfectly. That zeal on behalf of the suffering masses was nothing more nor less than disguised zeal on behalf of my own starved passions. I was poor and desperate. . . . I identified myself with the poor and ignorant; I did not make their cause my own, but my own cause theirs.

He became in fact, as *Demos* shows, an intransigent anti-socialist. For though for a time he lived among the very poor, he was never of them. His attitude towards them in the mass was one of outraged disgust and of real fear. It cannot be said that he was utterly devoid of pity for them; there is the unwontedly tender description in *Thyrza* of slum children dancing to a barrel-organ; but those of the poor who win his sympathy are essentially the exceptional among them, those most nearly akin temperamentally to himself—Grail, for instance, in the same novel, struggling to educate himself by reading the English classics (and, incidentally, bringing disaster upon himself as a consequence), and Bunce, the inarticulate atheist. But except in rare instances, almost always of women, he is unmoved by the humour, the kindliness, the courage of the poor, unmoved because he does not appear to have seen them. He saw only the brutishness and smelt only the smell: 'Personal uncleanliness made Slimy's proximity at all times unpleasant.'

But it is only in his early novels that Gissing concerns himself primarily with the condition of the people. Poverty remains a main theme, but it is no longer the poverty affecting masses; it is poverty as a crippling factor in the lives of what may be called naturally superior people whose fate it is to be born in the lower classes. Of such he wrote in *New Grub Street*: 'To the relatively poor (who are so much worse off than the poor absolutely) education is in most cases a mocking cruelty.' When these naturally superior people are men they are almost invariably manifestations of Gissing himself. Characteristic of them is Godwin Peak, the hero of *Born in Exile*. 'A militant egoist,' as we may assume that Gissing was, Peak is early and to an almost intolerable degree isolated from his family by his zeal for learning and his fierce ambition; but no less fierce than his ambition is his pride, and he throws up a brilliant career as a student at Whitelaw College (for which we may perhaps read Owens College, Manchester) because his vulgar uncle proposes to open an eating-house opposite the college gates. He goes to London, and in the course of time becomes an industrial chemist, but 'his one supreme desire', as he explains to a friend, 'is to marry a perfectly refined woman. Put it in the correct terms: I am a plebeian, and I aim at marrying a lady.' An arrogant rationalist, he writes an anonymous article ridiculing the pretensions of a popular book the purport of which is to reconcile science and religion. Then, when he recognizes the 'perfectly refined woman' of his desire, in order to ingratiate himself with her and her wealthy father he quite cynically avows his intention of studying for ordination and plans for himself a distinguished career as an Anglican parson. Exposed, he dies alone in exile in Switzerland,[1] having inherited too late the fortune of a woman who loved him.

By any standard, Peak is a remarkable piece of characterization. In the conviction he carries and in the impression he creates of outstanding intellectual ability, he calls irresistibly to mind Turgenev's Bazarov, and it is the index of Gissing's achievement that Peak is not extinguished by the comparison.

But the character is greater than the book, for Gissing is less successful in his scenes of upper-class life. His representations of *milieux* in which graciousness and culture are taken for granted have always the thinness of a dream world. Like so many novelists, he was inspired more by what he hated than by what he loved, and a more consistently successful novel is *New Grub Street*, surely the most bitter depiction of the calamities of authors ever composed. *New Grub Street* contains two of Gissing's finest women characters, Amy Reardon and Marian Yule, and two of his best studies of marriage

[1] In Vienna. (P. C. 1967.)

As a delineator of men his range was limited in the main to men like himself, idealists at odds with life, thwarted by poverty or the consciousness of ambitions and talents beyond their means and class. It was for women that he reserved his sympathy and compassion, and the memorable women of his novels are much more numerous and more varied than the men. But he distinguished very carefully between women. He writes in *Born in Exile*: 'Godwin was one of those upon whose awakening intellect is forced a perception of the brain-defect so general in women when they are taught few of life's graces and none of its serious concerns—their paltry prepossessions, their vulgar sequaciousness, their invincible ignorance, their absorption in a petty self.' Similar views are expressed throughout his work. One might have expected, especially in view of his own disastrous early marriages, a misogynic note in Gissing. It is true that no novelist has rendered more surely than he the miseries of matrimony as they arise from woman's jealousy, shrewishness or sluttishness. One remembers Harriet Casti in *The Unclassed*, in whom all those qualities are combined. Yet the same novel has one of his most charming heroines, Ida Starr, the young prostitute, in whom with the utmost skill he shows not only real intellectual ability but also the growth of spiritual and moral graciousness. Then there is *Thyrza*, his tenderest novel, with its three contrasted heroines of the slums, Thyrza and Lydia Trent and Totty Nancarrow. He has written scarcely a novel which does not contain a notable woman character.

His finest works are probably *The Odd Women* and *In the Year of Jubilee*. Neither contains a male character to match Peak in *Born in Exile* or Reardon in *New Grub Street*, but neither is marred by the special pleading and self-pity which accompany these partial self-portraits; and there is, too, a measure of detachment such as Gissing does not elsewhere attain. Both are concerned with women and the woman's problem of the day. In *The Odd Women* Gissing attacks the problem directly; a later novelist might have called the novel *The Surplus Women*, for essentially the theme is the fate of women who do not possess economic security. How should they arrange their lives? He presents the problem in terms of the three daughters of an improvident doctor, who leaves them with the tiniest of legacies and without training of any kind. With these is contrasted Rhoda Nunn, an impassioned feminist who conceives it her task in life to prepare women for an active role apart from marriage. It is Gissing's most objective novel, the nearest to the work of the French naturalists that he wrote, a most impressive study of loneliness in

London lodgings, of women maintaining middle-class respectability on the minimum of means. In it he exhibited the fate of the 'unwanted' middle-class Victorian woman in all her heroism and pathos —he wrote nothing more moving than his vignette of the secret gin-drinker Virginia Madden—and the effect is the stronger because of his restraint and detachment.

Woman, rather than the woman's problem, is the subject of *In the Year of Jubilee*, the most controlled expression of Gissing's disgust at his age that he was ever to achieve. The vulgarity of that age is exposed, sometimes overtly, as in the descriptions of the Jubilee crowds or in the following:

> Sitting opposite to Samuel, she avoided his persistent glances by reading the rows of advertisements above his head. Somebody's 'Blue'; somebody's 'Soap'; somebody's 'High-class Jams'; and, behold, inserted between the Soap and the Jam—'God so loved the world that He gave His only-begotten Son, that whosoever believeth in Him should not perish, but have everlasting life';

and sometimes in a wintry comedy, as with Samuel Barmby, with his 'Carlyle and Gurty! Yes, Carlyle and Gurty; those two authors are an education in themselves.' The vulgarity is presented, too, in three of Gissing's most appalling women, Beatrice and Fanny French and their sister Ada Peachey, whose 'features resembled Fanny's, but had a much less amiable expression, and betokened, if the thing were possible, an inferior intellect.' But the novel contains also one of his most successful heroines; Nancy Lord is not in the least idealized, indeed in the early chapters she is almost as unpromising human material as the Frenches themselves, but she yet develops through her tribulations a strength of moral character which enables her to make a success of a marriage that at first seemed utterly disastrous.

'To write of Gissing,' said Mr. Swinnerton more than thirty-five years ago in what is still the only full-length study of the novelist we have, 'is to write of one who failed.' But this is true only if he is judged by the highest standards. We must accept him as he was. He gave us a unique picture of the England of his time, a picture composed by one who felt himself always in exile. It is valuable because it is of its time, but it is valuable for another reason also. So long as there is a class system, whatever the nature of the system may be, there will be men and women who do not find themselves at home in any class, who feel themselves permanently estranged, at odds with society, and therefore isolated in the loneliness which the uprooted must always feel. Such men and women—and there are certainly no fewer today than there were sixty years ago—will find the mirror-image of their situation in all its bitterness in Gissing's strong, sombre, impassioned novels.

5

George Gissing[*][1]

GEORGE ORWELL

IN the shadow of the atomic bomb it is not easy to talk confidently about progress. However, if it can be assumed that we are *not* going to be blown to pieces in about ten years' time, there are many reasons, and George Gissing's novels are among them, for thinking that the present age is a good deal better than the last one. If Gissing were still alive he would be younger than Bernard Shaw, and yet already the London of which he wrote seems almost as distant as that of Dickens. It is the fog-bound, gas-lit London of the 'eighties, a city of drunken puritans, where clothes, architecture and furniture had reached their rock-bottom of ugliness, and where it was almost normal for a working-class family of ten persons to inhabit a single room. On the whole Gissing does not write of the worst depths of poverty, but one can hardly read his descriptions of lower-middle class life, so obviously truthful in their dreariness, without feeling that we have improved perceptibly on that black-coated, money-ruled world of only sixty years ago.

Everything of Gissing's—except perhaps one or two books written towards the end of his life—contains memorable passages, and anyone who is making his acquaintance for the first time might do worse than start with *In Year of Jubilee*. It was rather a pity, however, to use up paper in reprinting two of his minor works[2] when the books by which he ought to be remembered are and have been for years completely unprocurable. *The Odd Women*, for instance, is about as thoroughly out of print as a book can be. I possess a copy myself, in one of those nasty little red-covered cheap editions

* Reprinted from the *London Magazine*, June 1960, pp. 36-43, by permission of the editors.

[1] This article was originally commissioned for a magazine which came to an end before it could be published. It has only recently come to light again.

[2] *In Year of Jubilee* and *The Whirlpool*.

that flourished before the 1914 war, but that is the only copy I have ever seen or heard of *New Grub Street*, Gissing's masterpiece, I have never succeeded in buying. When I have read it, it has been in soup-stained copies borrowed from public lending libraries: so also with *Demos, The Nether World* and one or two others. So far as I know only *The Private Papers of Henry Ryecroft*, the book on Dickens, and *A Life's Morning*, have been in print at all recently. However, the two now reprinted are well worth reading, especially *In Year of Jubilee*, which is the more sordid and therefore the more characteristic.

In his introduction Mr. William Plomer remarks that 'generally speaking, Gissing's novels are about money and women', and Miss Myfanwy Evans says something very similar in introducing *The Whirlpool*. One might, I think, widen the definition and say that Gissing's novels are a protest against the form of self-torture that goes by the name of respectability. Gissing was a bookish, perhaps over-civilized man, in love with classical antiquity, who found himself trapped in a cold, smoky, Protestant country where it was impossible to be comfortable without a thick padding of money between yourself and the outer world. Behind his rage and querulousness there lay a perception that the horrors of life in late-Victorian England were largely unnecessary. The grime, the stupidity, the ugliness, the sex-starvation, the furtive debauchery, the vulgarity, the bad manners, the censoriousness—these things were unnecessary, since the puritanism of which they were a relic no longer upheld the structure of society. People who might, without becoming less efficient, have been reasonably happy chose instead to be miserable, inventing senseless taboos with which to terrify themselves. Money was a nuisance not merely because without it you starved; what was more important was that unless you had quite a lot of it—£300 a year, say—society would not allow you to live gracefully or even peacefully. Women were a nuisance because even more than men they were the believers in taboos, still enslaved to respectability even when they had offended against it. Money and women were therefore the two instruments through which society avenged itself on the courageous and the intelligent. Gissing would have liked a little more money for himself and some others, but he was not much interested in what we should now call social justice. He did not admire the working class as such, and he did not believe in democracy. He wanted to speak not for the multitude, but for the exceptional man, the sensitive man, isolated among barbarians.

In *The Odd Women* there is not a single major character whose life is not ruined either by having too little money, or by getting it too late in life, or by the pressure of social conventions which are obviously absurd but which cannot be questioned. An elderly spinster crowns a useless life by taking to drink; a pretty young girl marries a man old enough to be her father; a struggling schoolmaster puts off marrying his sweetheart until both of them are middle-aged and withered; a good-natured man is nagged to death by his wife; an exceptionally intelligent, spirited man misses his chance to make an adventurous marriage and relapses into futility; in each case the ultimate reason for the disaster lies in obeying the accepted social code, or in not having enough money to circumvent it. In *A Life's Morning* an honest and gifted man meets with ruin and death because it is impossible to walk about a big town with no hat on. His hat is blown out of the window when he is travelling in the train, and as he had not enough money to buy another, he misappropriates some money belonging to his employer, which sets going a series of disasters. This is an interesting example of the changes in outlook that can suddenly make an all-powerful taboo seem ridiculous. Today, if you had somehow contrived to lose your trousers, you would probably embezzle money rather than walk about in your underpants. In the 'eighties the necessity would have seemed equally strong in the case of a hat. Even thirty or forty years ago, indeed, bareheaded men were booed at in the street. Then, for no very clear reason, hatlessness became respectable, and today the particular tragedy described by Gissing—entirely plausible in its context—would be quite impossible.

The most impressive of Gissing's books is *New Grub Street*. To a professional writer it is also an upsetting and demoralizing book, because it deals among other things with that much-dreaded occupational disease, sterility. No doubt the number of writers who suddenly lose the power to write is not large, but it is a calamity that *might* happen to anybody at any moment, like sexual impotence. Gissing, of course, links it up with his habitual themes—money, the pressure of the social code, and the stupidity of women.

Edwin Reardon, a young novelist—he has just deserted a clerkship after having a fluky success with a single novel—marries a charming and apparently intelligent young woman, with a small income of her own. Here, and in one or two other places, Gissing makes what now seems the curious remark that it is difficult for an educated man who is not rich to get married. Reardon brings it off, but his less successful friend, who lives in an attic and supports himself by ill-paid tutoring jobs, has to accept celibacy as a matter of course. If he did succeed in finding himself a wife, we are told, it could only be an uneducated girl from the slums. Women of refinement and sensibility will not face poverty. And here one notices again the deep difference between that day and our own. Doubtless Gissing is right in implying all through his books that intelligent women are very rare animals; and if one wants to marry a woman who is intelligent *and* pretty, then the choice is still further restricted, according to a well-known arithmetical rule. It is like being allowed to choose only among albinos, and left-handed albinos at that. But what comes out in Gissing's treatment of his odious heroine, and of certain others among his women, is that at that date the idea of delicacy, refinement, even intelligence, in the case of a woman, was hardly separable from the idea of superior social status and expensive physical surroundings. The sort of woman whom a writer would want to marry was also the sort of woman who would shrink from living in an attic. When Gissing wrote *New Grub Street* that was probably true, and it could, I think, be justly claimed that it is not true today.

Almost as soon as Reardon is married it becomes apparent that his wife is merely a silly snob, the kind of woman in whom 'artistic tastes' are no more than a cover for social competitiveness. In marrying a novelist she has thought to marry someone who will rapidly become famous and shed reflected glory upon herself. Reardon is a studious, retiring, ineffectual man, a typical Gissing hero. He has been caught up in an expensive, pretentious world in which he knows he will never be able to maintain himself, and his nerve fails almost immediately. His wife, of course, has not the faintest understanding of what is meant by literary creation. There is a terrible passage—terrible, at least, to anyone who earns his living by writing—in which she calculates the number of pages that it would be possible to write in a day, and hence the number of novels that her husband may be expected to produce in a year—with the reflection that really it is not a very laborious profession. Meanwhile Reardon has been stricken dumb. Day after day he sits at his desk; nothing happens, nothing comes. Finally, in panic, he manufactures a piece of rubbish; his publisher, because Reardon's previous book had been successful, dubiously accepts it. Thereafter he is unable to produce anything that even looks as if it might be printable. He is finished.

The desolating thing is that if only he could get back to his clerkship and his bachelorhood, he would be all right. The hard-boiled journalist who finally marries Reardon's widow sums him up accurately by saying that he is the kind of man who, if left to himself, would write a fairly good book every two years. But, of course, he is not left to himself. He cannot revert to his old profession, and he cannot simply settle down to live on his wife's money: public opinion, operating through his wife, harries him into impotence and finally into the grave. Most of the other literary characters in the book are not much more fortunate, and the troubles that beset them are still very much the same today. But at least it is unlikely that the book's central disaster would now happen in quite that way or for quite those reasons. The chances are that Reardon's wife would be less of a fool, and that he would have fewer scruples about walking out on her if she made life intolerable for him. A woman of rather similar type turns up in *The Whirlpool* in the person of Alma Frothingham. By contrast there are the three Miss Frenches in *In the Year of Jubilee*, who represent the emerging lower-middle class —a class which, according to Gissing, was getting hold of money and power which it was not fitted to use—and who are quite surprisingly coarse, rowdy, shrewish and unmoral. At first sight Gissing's 'ladylike' and 'unladylike' women seem to be different and even opposite kinds of animal, and this seems to invalidate his implied condemnation of the female sex in general. The connecting link between them, however, is that all of them are miserably limited in outlook. Even the clever and spirited ones, like Rhoda in *The Odd Women* (an interesting early specimen of the New Woman), cannot think in terms of generalities, and cannot get away from ready-made standards. In his heart Gissing seems to feel that women are natural inferiors. He wants them to be better educated, but on the other hand, he does not want them to have freedom, which they are certain to misuse. On the whole the best women in his books are the self-effacing, home-keeping ones.

There are several of Gissing's books that I have never read, because I have never been able to get hold of them, and these unfortunately include *Born in Exile*, which is said by some people to be his best book. But merely on the strength of *New Grub Street*, *Demos* and *The Odd Women* I am ready to maintain that England has produced very few better novelists. This perhaps sounds like a rash statement until one stops to consider what is meant by a novel. The word 'novel' is commonly used to cover almost any kind of story—*The Golden Asse*, *Anna Karenina*, *Don Quixote*, *The Improvisatore*, *Madame Bovary*, *King Solomon's Mines* or anything else you like—but it also has a narrower sense in which it means something hardly existing before the nineteenth century and flourishing chiefly in Russia and France. A novel, in this sense, is a story which attempts to describe credible human beings, and—without necessarily using the technique of naturalism—to show them acting on everyday motives and not merely undergoing strings of improbable adventures. A true novel, sticking to this definition, will also contain at least two characters, probably more, who are described from the inside and on the same level of probability—which, in effect, rules out the novels written in the first person. If one accepts this definition, it becomes apparent that the novel is not an art-form in which England has excelled. The writers commonly paraded as 'great English novelists' have a way of turning out either to be not true novelists, or not to be Englishmen. Gissing was not a writer of picaresque tales, or burlesques, or comedies, or political tracts: he was interested in individual human beings, and the fact that he can deal sympathetically with several different sets of motives, and make a credible story out of the collision between them, makes him exceptional among English writers.

Certainly there is not much of what is usually called beauty, not much lyricism, in the situations and characters that he chooses to imagine, and still less in the texture of his writing. His prose, indeed, is often disgusting. Here are a couple of samples:

> Not with impunity could her thought accustom itself to stray in regions forbidden, how firm soever her resolve to hold bodily aloof. (*The Whirlpool.*)
>
> The ineptitude of uneducated English women in all that relates to their attire is a fact that it boots not to enlarge upon. (*In the Year of Jubilee.*)

However, he does not commit the faults that really matter. It is always clear what he means, he never 'writes for effect', he knows how to keep the balance between récit and dialogue and how to make dialogue sound probable while not contrasting too sharply with the prose that surrounds it. A much more serious fault than his inelegant manner of writing is the smallness of his range of experience. He is only acquainted with a few strata of society, and, in spite of his vivid understanding of the pressure of circumstance on character, does not seem to have much grasp of political or economic forces. In a mild way his outlook is reactionary, from lack of foresight rather than from ill-will. Having been obliged to live among them, he regarded the working class as savages, and in saying so he was merely being intellectually honest; he did not see that they were capable of becoming civilized if given slightly better opportunities. But, after all, what one demands from a novelist is not prophecy, and part of the charm of Gissing is that he belongs so unmistakably to his own time, although his time treated him badly.

The English writer nearest to Gissing always seems to be his contemporary, or near-contemporary, Mark Rutherford. If one simply tabulates their outstanding qualities, the two men appear to be very different. Mark Rutherford was a less prolific writer than Gissing, he was less definitely a novelist, he wrote much better prose, his books belong less recognizably to any particular time, and he was in outlook a social reformer and, above all, a puritan. Yet there is a sort of haunting resemblance, probably explained by the fact that both men lack that curse of English writers, a 'sense of humour'. A certain low-spiritedness, and air of loneliness, is common to both of them. There are, of course, funny passages in Gissing's books but he is not chiefly concerned with getting a laugh—above all, he has no impulse towards burlesque. He treats all his major characters more or less seriously, and with at least an attempt at sympathy. Any novel will inevitably contain minor characters who are mere grotesques or who are observed in a purely hostile spirit, but there is such a thing as impartiality, and Gissing is more capable of it than the great majority of English writers. It is a point in his favour that he had no very strong moral purpose. He had, of course, a deep loathing of the ugliness, emptiness and cruelty of the society he lived in, but he was concerned to describe it rather than to change it. There is usually no one in his books who can be pointed to as the villain, and even when there is a villain he is not punished. In his treatment of sexual matters Gissing is surprisingly frank, considering the time at which he was writing. It is not that he writes pornography or expresses approval of sexual promiscuity, but simply that he is willing to face the facts. The unwritten law of English fiction, the law that the hero as well as the heroine of a novel should be virgin when married, is disregarded in his books, almost for the first time since Fielding.

Like most English writers subsequent to the mid-nineteenth century, Gissing could not imagine any desirable destiny other than being a writer or a gentleman of leisure. The dichotomy between the intellectual and the lowbrow already existed, and a person capable of writing a serious novel could no longer picture himself as fully satisfied with the life of a business-man, or a soldier, or a politician, or what-not. Gissing did not, at least consciously, even want to be the kind of writer that he was. His ideal, a rather melancholy one, was to have a moderate private income and live in a small comfortable house in the country, preferably unmarried, where he could wallow in books, especially the Greek and Latin classics. He might perhaps have realized this ideal if he had not managed to get himself into prison immediately after winning an Oxford scholarship: as it was he spent his life in what appeared to him to be hackwork) and when he had at last reached the point where he could stop writing against the clock, he died almost immediately, aged only about forty-five. His death, described by H. G. Wells in his *Experiment in Autobiography*, was of a piece with his life. The twenty novels, or thereabouts, that he produced between 1880 and 1900 were, so to speak, sweated out of him during his struggle towards a leisure which he never enjoyed and which he might not have used to good advantage if he had had it: for it is difficult to believe that his temperament really fitted him for a life of scholarly research. Perhaps the natural pull of his gifts would in any case have drawn him towards novel-writing sooner or later. If not, we must be thankful for the piece of youthful folly which turned him aside from a comfortable middle-class career and forced him to become the chronicler of vulgarity, squalor and failure.

6

*Gissing's Heroines**

IN *Old Calabria*, Norman Douglas, who admired 'the harmonious pages' of *By the Ionian Sea*, tells of his search for memories of Gissing in Cotrone. He found Dr. Sculco. 'Yes, I remember him well: the young English poet who was ill here.' . . .

It is hardly how those who still think of Gissing conceive him. He was, indeed, not quite forty when he sickened at Cotrone; and he had only six years more. The youth may be allowed; but the poet is unexpected. Yet that may well be how he struck the sympathetic doctor to whom he told the marvellous visions of the classical world that came to him during his fever. And there is more justification for it than that. In the sense of Yeats's dictum, 'Out of our quarrels with ourselves we make poetry,' Gissing's novels represent a poetic achievement.

All through his life Gissing took refuge from the sordid and disheartening present in the classical past; but even there, partly through the influence of Gibbon, partly for deeper reasons, his predilection was for the Roman Empire in its decline. Memories of Cassiodorus no less than the older glories of Magna Graecia led him to the shores of the Ionian Sea. His literary career began with a prize poem on Ravenna and ended with an unfinished novel of the struggle between Byzantines and Goths for Italy. *Veranilda* is, on the whole, a dim book; but the chapters describing Basil's sojourn at Monte Cassino persist in the memory. More than Gissing's antiquarian imagination was at work in them: an anxious spiritual concern with the possibility that the religious life was the only source whence the continuity of civilization could be maintained and its forces replenished. Basil acknowledges that the peace of Monte Cassino is due to the absence of woman; but he is in love and not only finds justification for himself, but receives the blessing of Benedict on his earthly vocation.

It is a conscious parable of Gissing's life, and an epitome of his thinking. Continually, in his novels, he puts the question: 'On what,

* *The Times Literary Supplement*, 28 December 1956, p. 780.

given the inevitable decay of dogmatic religion, can an effective morality be based?' He has one answer. Salvation, though only for the few, is to be found in truth and love; truth in facing the facts of existence; love—primarily between man and woman—in inspiring individuals to contend against them. His idiosyncrasy is that he embodies this latter ideal almost exclusively in the figures of women. Emily Hood, in *A Life's Morning*, may serve, in this sole respect, for the pattern of all his heroines.

> Far removed from the world which theorizes, she presented in her character a solution of the difficulties entertained by those who doubtingly seek a substitute for the old religious sanctions. Her motives had the simplicity of elemental faith; they were indeed but the primary instincts of womanhood exalted to a rare perfection and reflected in a consciousness of exceeding lucidity.

That is not to imply that there is monotony in Gissing's women. The very contrary is true. They are remarkably various. Indeed, the most striking thing about his novels—in this matter like Hardy's—is the number of his persuasive women compared to the fewness of his convincing men. Four only of his important men remain really vivid —Bernard Kingcote in *Isabel Clarendon*, Edwin Reardon in *New Grub Street*, Godwin Peak in *Born in Exile*, and Ross Mallard in *The Emancipated*—and they are all indubitably projections of various aspects of himself. But the number of his distinctive women is impressive indeed. Nor are they idealized; some embody the ideal, others are the antithesis of it, but all are measured by it. They range from pure horrors of animality and vindictiveness like Harriet Smales and Clem Peckover and Ada Peachey to exemplars of loyalty and devotion like Ida Starr and Sidwell Warricombe and Nancy Lord.

Towards the end of his life he was fascinated by the ambiguity of woman. Louise Derrick, Eve Madeley, Polly Sparkes, Rosamund Elvan—all these characters of his slighter and later novels have in them something of 'the passive strength of woman, that characteristic which at times makes her a force of nature rather than an individual being' which amazed the hero of *Will Warburton*. This amorality of so many women, their larger endowment with what Spinoza called the 'vis existendi', astonished and intrigued Gissing; and, within the limits imposed by the sexual convention of his time, he depicted it well, and with increasing fidelity. It is the quality in woman on which Bernard Shaw insisted; but Gissing, compelled by nature to much more intimate relations with women, was immune from Shaw's intellectual falsification of it. Where Shaw's women are puppets, Gissing's are alive. From Isabel Clarendon down to Polly Sparkes, their deep desire is to respect their men; and the recurrent pathos of the situation is that the men shrink from doing their duty. As it is with Bernard Kingcote, so it is with Edwin Reardon and Godwin Peak.

The nearest that Gissing comes to an imaginative resolution of the man-woman dilemma is in *The Emancipated*, where Mallard the painter eventually breaks down the puritanical inhibitions and overcomes the jealousies of Miriam Baske, and we are satisfied that a life of mutual fulfilment lies before them. But Mallard, unlike the typical Gissing hero, is sure of himself; devoted, after much rigorous self-examination, to what D. H. Lawrence called his 'male purpose'. And so few of Gissing's men are. Of those who are not proletarians, hard set to make a living at all, most are young men with independent incomes, large or small, who cannot make up their minds to do anything: the others are writers or artists, whether self-distrustful like Edwin Reardon, or doggedly confident like Mallard. This contrast between the insufficiency or shadowiness of his men and the reality of his women points to a peculiar bias of the imagination in Gissing.

The cause of this imaginative bias clearly lies in his own miserable experience of two utterly disastrous marriages. To call them merely unhappy would be a gross understatement: they were such marriages that either of them would have been enough to wreck the life of a sensitive man. But the first of them, at least, was obviously the outcome of a romantic idealism—the dangerous mixture of sexual attraction and a genuine desire to rescue the victim of circumstance. The full story of the second is still obscure: but it seems to have been the result of sex-starvation on a man too diffident, too poor and too proud to seek an equal mate—above all, too fearful of life, too deeply persuaded that the poverty he had to offer would lead to the degeneration of the kind of woman he desired: the destiny from which Bernard Kingcote flinches in *Isabel Clarendon* and which Edwin Reardon lives through in *New Grub Street*. But those two impressive books serve to show to what creative purpose Gissing turned his domestic disasters. And, lamentable though the fact may be, it is startlingly plain that it was only so long as his domestic misery endured that Gissing maintained the peculiar intensity of imagination that distinguishes his characteristic novels. After *Eve's Ransom* they no longer compel the reader into emotional participation in the destinies of their characters.

It is arguable that Gissing had simply exhausted himself, writing long novel after long novel in his wretched circumstances. But this does not account for the marked change in attitude in his later books. The women are no longer intensely conceived. Irene Derwent in *The Crown of Life* is, in one sense, as much an ideal woman as any of the previous gallery; but she is not realized, she satisfied no hunger of the imagination, the temperature of creation is lukewarm. And such minor creations as Polly Sparkes in *The Town Traveller* or Rosamund Elvan in *Will Warburton* or Louise Derrick in *The Paying Guest* have an altogether new note. They are women seen with an amused detachment, with a play of light and indulgent humour which is gratifying enough to those who have endured the storm and stress of the fortunes of Gissing's previous heroines. We are happy to think that he is no longer seriously involved, neither dreaming fulfilments nor foreboding disasters; and we suspect—what the biography bears out—that he is in sight of his quantum of domestic felicity. He wrote in *The Crown of Life*:

> For the men capable of passionate love (and they are few) to miss love is to miss everything. Life has but the mockery of consolation for that one gift denied. The heart may be dulled by time; it is not comforted. Illusion if it be, it is that which crowns all other illusions whereof life is made. The man must prove it, or he is born in vain.

The effort to prove it supplied the distinctive dynamic to Gissing's impressive work of imaginative creation.

It is idle to debate the question whether Gissing was, by nature, a novelist. He was a writer by nature; and he had to make a living. That he could have been a fine critic his book on Dickens proves: it is still the best criticism of Dickens extant. (It also proves, by the extraordinary vehemence of the chapter on Dickens's women, how hard it was for him to subdue the bitterness of his personal experience.) But he was determined not to waste his powers in journalism. He clung desperately to his intellectual integrity and artistic independence, when there was little else for him to cling to: writing novels, however meagrely rewarded, was the only way. He began with novels of the nether world, chiefly because his destiny had thrust him into it. He knew that world and he had a passion for veracity. And it enabled him to offer something new to the novel-reading public. As Henry James said, he was '*the* authority, in fact, on a region vast and unexplored'. But, since he was incapable of sentimentalizing it (or even of appreciating that its denizens were sometimes happy) and had nothing of Dickens's great gift of humorous caricature, the novel-reading public upon whom success depended found his books depressing and distasteful.

When he broke new ground, as he tried early to do in *Isabel Clarendon* and *A Life's Morning*, and ventured into a world of wealth and culture, inward veracity compelled him to deal with the strain of contact between it and educated poverty. Only by so doing could he make the situations psychologically real to himself, and worth labouring over. Again, he failed to please any but the few. So he returned, in *Demos* and *Thyrza* and *The Nether World*, to the more familiar environment, but carrying over into it, in the first two of these novels, the perplexing problem of contact between the classes. The grim story of Richard Mutimer's marriage to Adela Waltham is surpassed in imaginative appeal by the tragedy of Thyrza Trent's passion for Walter Egremont. But, just as before in *Isabel Clarendon* and *A Life's Morning*, Gissing tries first one way and then the other: the refined man with the poor woman, the refined woman with the working man. The peculiarity of *Thyrza* is that in order to make Thyrza credible (as he triumphantly does) Gissing endows nearly all the working-class characters with a native nobility of soul. Whether in reaction against this artistically justifiable idealization, or for some other cause, the next and last of his proletarian novels, *The Nether World*, is of squalor and misery almost unrelieved. Gissing put the screw on his most faithful reader. The contrast in emotional tone between *Thyrza* and *The Nether World* is astonishing; and it is highly probable that the cause must be sought in the emotional shock he received from the squalor and pathos of his first wife's death.

It was his farewell to the underworld. Understandably he moved clean away from it into the cultivated society of *The Emancipated*: in which he convincingly contrasts the swift decay of an illusory love-passion with the slow consolidation of a relation based on that 'highest love which is also highest reason'. *New Grub Street* and *Born in Exile* followed—probably the most familiar of Gissing's novels today, and certainly among his very best. Both are subtle, and both convincing explorations of love between educated poor man and refined woman, with the difference that in the former the flaw is in the woman, in the latter in the man. In both, exceptionally, the man is completely real; a successful objectification of two facets of the author's complex nature; while the women, Amy Reardon and Sidwell Warricombe, belong to his finest creations. Gissing had touched his pinnacle.

It is said that he wrote his next novel, *The Odd Women*, a full three-volume affair, in six weeks. Considered in that light, it is a *tour de force* indeed; but, though interesting, it is diffuse and lacks intensity. The wonder is that it is as good as it is, for the economic pressure on Gissing was crushing. While *Born in Exile* was going the round of reluctant publishers, he had had to jump at the offer by a new publisher of 100 guineas for a one-volume novel, *Denzil Quarrier*, which is as nearly worthless as anything he ever wrote. Next came three books, each with its own distinction. In *In the Year of Jubilee* he rid his bosom of much perilous stuff in the appalling picture of Ada Peachey—his second marriage was now a wreck—and comforted himself and his reader by the story of the delightful Nancy Lord's purgation into love. But beside her, her dilettante husband is a man of straw. *Eve's Ransom*, a *nouvelle* rather than a novel, is exquisite. On this scale, the man could be merely sketched with safety: and the whole point is that Eve Madeley is evasive. The ease and economy of Gissing's writing and his sureness of touch were then remarkable. And so they are in the suburban comedy of *The Paying Guest*, a delicate study of a vulgar but good-natured and not impercipient girl in search of refinement and a husband. This particular kind of exploration into the more common species of the eternal femininc is carried on in *The Town Traveller* and *Will Warburton* and to some extent in *Our Friend the Charlatan*. It is light-hearted, good-tempered, and above all detached: Gissing could, at last, smile at the human comedy. But when, in his one remaining serious novel, *The Whirlpool*, he tried to fill a big canvas with a picture of the corruption of upper-class society his failure was complete.

Because the book of Gissing's which has been most constantly reprinted is *The Private Papers of Henry Ryecroft*, and that has been misinterpreted as autobiography, it has been too easily assumed that Gissing was primarily a reflective essayist. And this impression has been strengthened by the relative, and deserved, popularity of *By the Ionian Sea*. But it is as a thinking novelist that he will be judged and remembered, so soon as his major novels are reprinted. There are at least a dozen of them which deserve it; and a comprehensive collected edition would not be inordinate. The faithful picture he gives of a London that is vanished like a bad dream should at least arouse nostalgia in the old and curiosity in the young. But his just claim to a minor immortality lies otherwhere.

7

*Division of Purpose in George Gissing**

JACOB KORG

MOST of George Gissing's social novels bear the mark of an allegiance divided between social reform and art. Each begins by addressing itself to some problem of nineteenth-century civilization, such as poverty, Mammonism, socialism, rack-renting, educational reform, or the position of women, depicting evil conditions with powerful social realism. As the novel proceeds, however, social questions are gradually relegated to the background, and the story becomes a steady and, at best, inevitable unfolding of events whose course is determined in the final analysis by the characters of the people involved in it. There may be frequent reversions to 'problems' and these may have some effect on the action, but a dénouement that fails to correspond with the social theme, or even contradicts it, makes it apparent that the novel of plot and character has usurped the place of the novel of protest. This inconsistency may well be one of the reasons why such social novels as *Workers in the Dawn* (1880), *The Unclassed* (1884), *Demos* (1886), *Thyrza* (1887), and *The Nether World* (1889) failed to win Gissing any but the smallest public, although they were recognized as faithful and moving portrayals of conditions that demanded reform.[1] One reviewer of *The Nether*

* Reprinted by permission of the Modern Language Association of America from PMLA Vol. LXX (1955), pp. 323-336.

[1] Frederic Harrison, after reading *Workers in the Dawn*, wrote enthusiastically of it to Gissing, saying: 'There can be no doubt as to the power of your book. It will take rank amongst the works of great rank of these years' (*Letters of George Gissing to Members of His Family*, London, 1931, letter of 23 July 1880). Charles Booth, explaining why his vast sociological report on the life of the poor was needed, said: 'It is not easy for any outsider to gain a sufficient insight into the lives of these people. The descriptions of them in the books we read are for the most part as unlike the truth as are descriptions of aristocratic life in the books they read. . . . Something may be gleaned from a few books, such as, for instance, "Demos" ' (*Life and Labour of the People in London*, 3rd ed., London and New York, 1892-97, I, 157).

World pointed clearly to the ambiguity characteristic of Gissing's work by saying: 'It is difficult to discover whether he hoped to add to that sort of fiction which has at times been more successful than Blue-books or societies in calling attention to evils crying for remedy or whether . . .the author chose his subject in something like an artistic spirit. . . . His work does not show the energy either of an artist or of an enthusiast . . .'[2]

The curious indecision of Gissing's novels has often been ascribed to a low level of vitality or responsiveness in the author.[3] However, if the chronicle of Gissing's diary is to be believed, he had to expend tremendous efforts to complete a novel, often beginning a book anew half a dozen times, or discarding unsatisfactory pages which represented weeks of work. He did not lack energy. On the contrary, the impulse to create and the impulse to reform were both vigorously at work in him, but through most of his career they contended with each other, subjecting his novels to a conflict of intentions in which the purposes of each were, to some extent, defeated. Why did Gissing fail to combine the two into some such union of art and ideas as that achieved by George Eliot, whom he admired, or by Ibsen, a contemporary whose work he found 'extraordinary'? An answer to this question and a cause for the puzzling inconsistencies of the novels are suggested by Gissing's attitude toward his work as it is revealed in the comments on art and fiction found in his books and letters.

Gissing reached intellectual maturity early, forming tastes and opinions as a youth which hardly changed when he became a man. While still a brilliant and precocious schoolboy he was impressed profoundly both by artistic and cultural tradition and by social injustice. He underwent a thorough education in the Greek and Latin classics, which he was to love throughout his life on purely aesthetic grounds. He also saw something of industrial poverty, probably in the manufacturing centres near his native town of Wakefield, for in 1871, at the age of fourteen, he wrote a poem which showed that the plight of the poor weighed heavily on his mind.[4]

[2] *Athenaeum*, 27 July 1889, p. 126.

[3] See, e.g., Frank Swinnerton's *George Gissing, A Critical Study* (London, 1912), and Q. D. Leavis in *Scrutiny*, VII (1938), 73-81.

[4] MS. Notebook, 'Verses 1869-[82],' Rare Book Room, Yale Univ. Library. The poem, which oddly anticipates Gissing's voyage to America, reads in part:

> Look upon the glorious ocean,
> Forward to the glorious West,

Two of the boy's favourite artists, Dickens and Hogarth, were moralists who used the life of the poor as subject matter. In an essay on Milton written as a school exercise when he was about fourteen, he expressed the opinion that poetry had a social function. 'Poetry', he wrote, 'is one of the great, and perhaps the greatest instrument of the education and enlightenment of the general public. . . . In many poems there is a great deal more truth than in many histories.'[5]

The experiences of his young manhood strengthened Gissing's concern with social problems and made it natural for him to choose them as material for his fiction. During his travels in the United States, when the publication of some short stories brought him his first modest success as a writer, he was never very far from destitution, and on his return to England in the fall of 1877 he entered on the life of precarious poverty so vividly described in *The Private Papers of Henry Ryecroft*. His sufferings were intensified by the irresponsible behaviour of his wife, a girl of the slums whom he married in the hope of educating and reforming.

During his first years in London after his return from America, Gissing was a poor young intellectual of revolutionary tendencies. He aligned himself politically with the Radicals, and after reading Comte's *Philosophie positive* became an enthusiastic Positivist. He was a sympathetic observer at a disorderly meeting of working men in Hyde Park in February of 1878, and in the following year addressed a club in Paddington on the subject of 'Faith and Reason', preparing himself for his talk by reading a number of leading rationalist works. The lecture was a great success, and he planned to speak again on 'The State Church from a Rationalist Point of View', but this second lecture was never delivered.[6] At the same time his feelings of rebellion were finding another and more significant outlet, for he was at work on a novel of protest which described poverty and its attendant evils with an overwhelming abundance of convincing episode and detail. After completing it he called it *Workers in the*

Far away from smoke and trouble,
  There is pleasure, *there* is rest. . . .
Then we'll think of one low island
  In the smoke and vapour roll'd
Think of struggling, toil-worn creatures,
  And we'll grudge them not their gold.

[5] MS. 'John Milton,' Berg Collection, New York Public Library.

[6] *Letters*, 23 March 1879. Some time later he was again preparing to speak on a political subject before a radical audience. See *Letters*, 24 April 1881.

Dawn, explaining his choice of this title to his brother by saying: 'It is a novel . . . of social questions, and the principal characters are earnest young people striving for improvement in, as it were, the dawn of a new phase of our civilization' (*Letters*, 2 January 1880). When it was published he explained its aims somewhat more fully: 'The book in the first place is not a novel in the generally-accepted sense of the word, but a very strong (possibly *too* plain spoken) attack upon certain features of our present religious and social life which to *me* appear highly condemnable. First and foremost, I attack the criminal negligence of governments which spend their time over matters of relatively no importance, to the neglect of the terrible social evils which should have been long since sternly grappled with. Herein I am a mouthpiece of the advanced Radical party' (8 June 1880).

Workers in the Dawn exposes the division of mind which was to haunt Gissing's career, for in spite of these avowals of the novel's propagandistic purpose, an important part of its plot is devoted to developing the idea that art should be free of propaganda. In describing the dilemma of the novel's protagonist, a young painter named Arthur Golding who is equally attracted to careers in art and social reform, Gissing was reviewing some of his own thoughts. He had evidently come under the influence of pre-Raphaelitism and aestheticism, for his character 'worships' beauty 'as a goddess' and Gissing himself admired Ruskin, Swinburne, Rossetti, and Morris. But like many of his contemporaries who would have preferred to spend their lives in the presence of beauty, Gissing felt that he could not be indifferent to the obvious evils of a distressed society. He shared fully the sense of moral responsibility described by Beatrice Webb as an important element in the literature, analytic thought, and religious activity of the time, and an animating force of the social reform movement in which she participated.[7] Ruskin, explaining why he turned from his aesthetic interests to the works on political economy which occupied the last part of his career, told of the common spiritual experience in personal and concrete terms: 'For my own part, I will put up with this state of things, passively, not an hour longer. I am not an unselfish person, nor an Evangelical one; I have no particular pleasure in doing good. . . . But I simply cannot paint, nor read, nor look at minerals, nor do anything else that I like, and the very light of the morning sky . . . has become hateful to me, because of the misery that I know of, and see signs

[7] Webb, *My Apprenticeship* (New York and London, 1926), pp. 173-177.

of, where I know it not, which no imagination can interpret too bitterly.[8]

In *Workers in the Dawn* the claims of the social conscience are urged on Arthur by his guardian, an elderly printer who tells him to emulate Hogarth by using his talent as an artist to reveal the ills of his age. But Arthur feels that art and social reform are incompatible with each other, and that he must ultimately make a choice of one of them. He finds his problem set forth in Tennyson's 'Palace of Art', which he reads in company with the woman he loves, Helen Norman. The allegory of an artist's soul taking refuge in a vast and beautiful palace only to be reminded of the suffering world outside by sinister intruding ghosts epitomizes Arthur's own division of mind. Helen resolves his conflict, but not by counselling him to follow the course implied in Tennyson's poem. She has read Shelley, and she gives Arthur a brief exposition of ideas drawn from 'A Defence of Poetry', telling him that art is the real source of morality, and that active social reform accomplishes little in comparison with it. Social workers like herself do some good, she says, 'but what is this compared with the labour of men of genius, labour the result of which stands as milestones on the highway of civilization?' Of the spirit governing their own time she says: 'that spirit itself was created by the great men whose works, howsoever performed, direct the history of the world. . . . You say that a beautiful picture only pleases its painter and a few rich *dilettanti*. In appearance it may do more, but in reality its spirit permeates every layer of society . . . nothing in this world is more useful than the beautiful, nothing works so powerfully for the ultimate benefit of mankind.[9]

The fact that Helen Norman speaks not merely in character, but also to express Gissing's own opinions is attested by the many

[8] Ruskin, Letter 1, '*Fors Clavigera,*' *Works* (New York, 1894), I, 4.

[9] These remarks from *Workers in the Dawn,* 2nd ed. (Garden City, 1935) II, 268-269, should be compared with the following passages of 'A Defence of Poetry': 'But poets, or those who imagine and express this indestructible order, are not only the authors of language and of music, of the dance, and architecture, and statuary, and painting; they are the institutors of laws and the founders of civil society, and the inventors of the arts of life. . . . Poets, according to the circumstances of the age and nation in which they appeared, were called, in the earlier epochs of the world, legislators or prophets: a poet essentially comprises and unites both these characters' (*Prose Works,* ed. Harry Buxton Forman, London, 1880, III, 103-104). 'Poets are the hierophants of an unapprehended inspiration; the mirrors of the gigantic shadows which futurity casts upon the present . . . the influence which is moved not, but moves. Poets are the unacknowledged legislators of the world' (*ibid.*, p. 144).

parallels with 'A Defence of Poetry' found among his ideas. Shelley attributed the poet's great power to his ability to perceive and exploit the principles governing society: 'the pleasure resulting from the manner in which they [poets] express the influence of society or nature upon their own minds, communicates itself to others, and gathers a sort of reduplication from the community' (p. 103). This conception of an intimate and mutual dependence between artist and society is found in Mr. Tollady's advice to Arthur in his long speeches about art and history in *Workers in the Dawn*, and in a speech of Waymark in *The Unclassed* (London, 1895), who answers the objection that his novels are didactic by saying: 'Every strong individuality is more or less the expression of its age. This direction may be imposed upon me; for all that, I understand why I pursue it' (p. 212). Gissing once wrote to his sister that while political ravings are soon forgotten, 'the works of the artist, work in what material he will, remain sources of health to the world' (*Letters*, 12 May 1883).

Gissing shared with Shelley the view that art was ethical by nature, and strengthened the moral sense. Shelley had said: 'A man, to be greatly good, must imagine intensely and comprehensively; he must put himself in the place of another and of many others; the pains and pleasures of his species must become his own. The great instrument of moral good is the imagination. . . . Poetry strengthens the faculty which is the organ of the moral nature of man, in the same manner as exercise strengthens a limb' (pp. 111-12). Gissing found in this theory an explanation of the difference in morality between the poor and other classes. The beauty, comfort, or variety in the daily lives of rich and middle-class people cultivated and enriched the imagination, providing a basis for the understanding of ethical ideas. In his novels art becomes a force which actually enables characters to rise above their limitations. *The Emancipated* (1890), for example, has a young Dissenting widow named Miriam Baske whose religious principles have driven her to retire into the loneliness of her Naples hotel room. But through the influence of an artist who espouses militantly aesthetic principles, and the effects of Italian art and literature, she learns to open herself to feelings, and to fall in love. Similarly, in *A Life's Morning* (1888) the heroine, a governess from a poor northern manufacturing town, is clearly aware that the tasteful appointments of her employer's country home have a calming and enriching influence upon her. Because of their narrowness of experience and ignorance of beauty, the poor, in Gissing's view, had no opportunities for learning a true morality. 'The fatal defect in working people is the absence of imagination, the power which may be solely a gift of nature and irrespective of circumstances, but which in most of us owes so much to intellectual training. Half the brutal cruelties perpetrated by uneducated men and women are directly traceable to lack of the imaginative spirit, which comes to mean lack of kindly sympathy.'[10]

Poetry, though essentially moral, must not, according to Shelley, attempt to teach morality directly, for that would limit its universality: 'A poet therefore would do ill to embody his own conceptions of right and wrong, which are usually those of his place and time, in his practical creations. . . . Those in whom the poetical faculty, though great, is less intense, as Euripides, Lucan, Tasso, Spenser, have frequently affected a moral aim, and the effect of their poetry is diminished in exact proportion to the degree in which they compel us to advert to this purpose' (p. 112). None of the doctrines of 'A Defence of Poetry' made a profounder impression on Gissing than this idea that overt moral teaching was a corruption of art. He made it one of his own opinions, and often stated it, in one form or another, in explaining critical judgments. It can be recognized in this comment on a character in *The Unclassed*: 'her soul in reality was that of an artist, and, whereas the artist should be free from everything like moral prepossession, Maud's aesthetic sensibilities were in perpetual conflict with her moral convictions' (p. 150). Writing to his German friend, Eduard Bertz, to whom he often confided his intellectual and artistic problems, he said: 'Yes, art must be typical; it does not deal in isolated manifestations—at all events not in such as suggest a moral influence."[11] Again, disapproving of Tolstoy's 'What is Art?' which he had read in its French translation, he said: 'Tolstoi is simply Ruskin. Art to be judged from the moral standpoint.'[12]

The general principles of 'A Defence of Poetry' are embodied in the critical ideas expressed by Gissing in his short essay, 'The Place of Realism in Fiction', written in 1895, and in *Charles Dickens: A Critical Study* (1898). These also bear the imprint of another influence, however. In 1888 Gissing read Henry James's volume, *Partial Portraits*, which contained the essay 'The Art of Fiction', and the latter might well have struck him as an extension of Shelley's

[10] *Demos* (London: Dent, n.d.), p. 125.
[11] Letter of 3 August 1896, Yale Univ. Library.
[12] Letter to Bertz, 4 September 1898, Yale Univ. Library.

principles of poetry and art to the novel; 'questions of art', said James, 'are questions (in the widest sense) of execution; questions of morality are quite another affair'.[13] James said of fictional creation what Shelley had said of poetry, that it was ultimately a matter of individual personality: 'A novel is in its broadest definition a personal, a direct impression of life. . . . The execution belongs to the author alone; it is what is most personal to him, and we measure him by that' (pp. 384-5). Gissing's definition of realism reflects these views, even echoing their language. Realism, he said, is equal to uncompromising sincerity. The realist 'holds that truth, for the artist, is the impression produced on him, and that to convey this impression with entire sincerity is his sole reason for existing'.[14] Since every artist experiences only a part of actuality and therefore beholds 'a world of his own', his work must inevitably be subjective. James said that the laws of fiction, if they did exist, were too general to be of much use as a guide to the writer, and Gissing concurred, saying more bluntly: 'There is no science of fiction.'[15] He felt that although it was possible to have an indefinite number of types of realism, Dickens could not be termed a realist, for he distorted the material he drew from life in order to make it suit his system of morality. Gissing's strict doctrine of realism parallels 'A Defence of Poetry' in two ways; it stresses subjectivity, and it rules out didacticism.

Although Shelley's theories supplied Gissing with a justification for eliminating social concerns from his mind, he was unable to accept them as a practical guide in his work. On the contrary, they seem to have intensified his conflict by convincing him that his love of art and learning and his hatred of social injustice had irreconcilable implications. It is astonishing to find that only a week after describing his first novel as 'a very strong . . . attack upon certain features of our present religious and social life' he complained of a reviewer who criticized its ideas as 'an amalgam of Schopenhauer, Comte and Shelley' on these grounds: 'he treats it too much as if it were a mere polemical pamphlet, and not a *work of art*, as which, of course, I desire it to be judged.'[16] Yet six months later, finding that

[13] (London and New York, 1894), p. 405.

[14] *Charles Dickens: A Critical Study* (London, 1898), p. 91.

[15] *Selections Autobiographical and Imaginative from the Works of George Gissing* (New York, 1929), p. 220.

[16] *Letters*, 15 June 1880. The offending review, the first of any work by Gissing, appeared in the *Athenaeum*, 12 June 1880.

Workers in the Dawn had failed to sell or bring him fame, he expressed his determination to continue both with fiction and with social protest, declaring himself in words that have the ring of a manifesto: 'I mean to bring home to people the ghastly condition (material, mental, and moral) of our poor classes, to show the hideous injustice of our whole system of society, to give light upon the plan of altering it, and, above all, to preach an enthusiasm for just and high *ideals* in this age of unmitigated egotism and "shop". I shall never write a book which does not keep all these ends in view' (*Letters*, 3 November 1880). He wrote polemics as well as novels, and was at one time almost ready to give up fiction in order to express his ideas more directly in the form of essays. 'I think there is little doubt', he wrote to his brother on 6 October 1882, 'that my work will ultimately follow the line which has been hinted at all along, I mean that of philosophico-social speculation. I feel more inclination at present to write in this abstract way than to go on embodying theories in fiction.'

This interest in social problems alternated, however, with moods of discouragement in which, despairing of the efficacy of social reform, he turned to the consolations of art. In a letter to one of his sisters he confessed that while he was dubious of Ruskin's practical reform theories, he agreed with those of his ideas which corresponded with aestheticism and Shelley's conception of the social role of art: 'His worship of Beauty I look upon as essentially valuable. . . . I am growing to feel, that the only thing known to us of absolute value is artistic perfection' (12 May 1883). At the beginning of his first extended Continental journey Gissing was forced to take up quarters at the Hôtel Roma of Rue Linné in a working-class section of Paris. Repelled by the spectacle of the poor in the surrounding streets, he entered in his diary a decision to devote himself to other things while he was away from London: 'I experience at present a profound dislike for everything that concerns the life of the people. . . . All my interest in such things I have left behind in London. On crossing the Channel, I have become a poet pure and simple, or perhaps it would be better to say an idealist student of art.'[17]

Gissing was supported in his adherence to the doctrines of 'A Defence of Poetry' by the growing aestheticism of the eighties, more particularly by that branch of it which held that art served the needs of the world best by occupying itself with purely artistic ends. The

[17] Holograph Diary, Berg Collection, New York Public Library, entry of 19 October 1888.

moral aesthetic of Ruskin, Arnold's view that culture acted as an ordering principle in civilization, and Morris's doctrine that art could be a powerful instrument of direct social reform were all attempts to win for art and cultural activities generally the recognition as formative influences on intellect and character which Shelley had claimed for them. Although he rejected all other social remedies advanced by his contemporaries, Gissing did share these views to a considerable extent, agreeing most nearly with Arnold. He felt that if the salvation of society were ever achieved, it would come about through the efforts of individuals isolated from the world's materialism who cultivated their finest faculties by the disinterested study of art and culture. This conviction was based on his own delight in study and reading. He often reported that he felt his spiritual resources strengthened by an evening with the classics, or by Dante, whom he read while teaching himself Italian, or by communion with great works of art and remains of the past in Greece and Italy. In the course of the week he spent examining the collections of the Vatican Museum he entered the following observation in his diary: 'Woke early this morning and enjoyed wonderful happiness of mind. It occurs to me, is not this partly due to the fact that I spend my days solely in the consideration of beautiful things, wholly undisturbed by base necessities and considerations? In any case the experience is most remarkable' (*Letters*, 14 December 1888).

Gissing's discouragement with the disorder of social and political life might often have taken the temporary form of an indifference resembling artistic detachment, but when he set himself to write a novel, a task made especially arduous for him by difficulties of temperament, it was in response to motivations that had little to do with detachment or aesthetic effects. The nature of the relationship between his love of art and his concern with social evils is briefly but sharply revealed in one of the protestations of his devotion to pure beauty that occur so often in his letters: 'When I am able to summon any enthusiasm at all,' he wrote to one of his sisters, 'it is only for ART—how I laughed the other day on recalling your amazement at my theories of Art for Art's sake! Well, I cannot get beyond it. Human life has little interest to me, on the whole—save as material for artistic presentation. I can get savage over social iniquities, but even then my rage at once takes the direction of planning revenge in artistic work' (12 June 1884). 'Revenge' was, in fact, often his most immediate aim in writing. When the publisher Bentley, after accepting his novel, *Mrs. Grundy's Enemies*, asked him to alter some parts which were found to be morally objectionable, he reluctantly complied, but promised to 'give it to the critics and the namby-pamby public' by writing a satire on their prudish tastes.[18] Even much later in his career he wrote with the aim of making a moral point, and repeatedly chose his subjects by fixing on some evil which he wanted to attack. He wrote to Bertz in 1892, describing a book he had in mind: 'It will present those people who, congenitally incapable of true education, have yet been taught to consider themselves too good for manual, or any humble, work.'[19] A similar theme was in his mind later in the same year: 'I want to deal with the flood of blackguardism which nowadays is pouring forth over the society which is raised by wealth above the lowest and yet is not sufficiently educated to rank with the highest. Impossible to take up a newspaper without being impressed with this fact of extending and deepening vulgarity.'[20] Once, after going to Worcestershire to gather material for a novel, he described his intentions thus: 'It is not my purpose to deal with the working-class of that district. I shall use it as a picturesque background to a story of middle-class life, insisting on the degree to which people have become *machines*, in harmony with the machinery amid which they spend their lives.'[21] Protesting against a critic who had found that the characters of *In the Year of Jubilee* (1894) were caricatures, Gissing again showed how he was guided by the desire to make a moral point: 'I have *selected* from the great mass of lower middle class life a group of people who represent certain of its grossnesses, weaknesses, etc., peculiar to our day.'[22]

Gissing's unwillingness to admit what his readers recognized immediately, that his novels were essentially didactic treatments of social themes which forcefully suggested the conclusions they withheld, was the cause of many misunderstandings between the writer and his public. The case of *The Unclassed* is typical. Among the novel's many didactic passages are some speeches by its novelist hero, Osmond Waymark, who, in the course of his pronouncements on art, philanthropy, and the materialism of the age, says that moral questions

[18] *Letters*, 14 February 1883. *Mrs Grundy's Enemies* was set up in type, and Gissing corrected the proofs, but it was never published and no copy of it is known today.

[19] Letter, 16 February 1892, Yale Univ. Library.

[20] Letter to Bertz, 1 May 1892, Yale Univ. Library.

[21] Letter to Bertz, 2 December 1892, Yale Univ. Library.

[22] MS. letter to Morley Roberts, 10 February 1895, Berg Collection, New York Public Library.

have little to do with the writer's task; he explains that the realism of his own work is not intended to arouse reform sentiment, but is simply a truthful artistic method. When a friend points out that Waymark, in spite of his doctrine that art should be independent of morality, continues to deal with social evils, he attributes the fact to the tenor of the times.

This exchange proved to be a rehearsal of the controversy that actually followed the publication of *The Unclassed*, with the difference that Gissing was unable to defend himself against criticism in actuality as well as he had in imagination. The *Athenaeum* reviewer, in his brief paragraph, declared that preaching was out of place in novels (28 June 1884, pp. 821-822). Frederic Harrison took violent issue with Waymark's opinions, calling them 'mere moral dynamite'. Even Gissing's brother pointed to an inconsistency (probably that between the hero's declared ideas and the outcome of the story), and Gissing hastened to explain what was certainly not clear in the novel: 'You evidently take Waymark's declaration of faith as my own. Now this is by no means the case. Waymark is a *study of character*, and he alone is responsible for his sentiments. Do you not perceive this in the very fact of that *contradiction* in the book of which you speak? . . . And I repeat it is not a social essay, but a study of a certain group of human beings. Of course, I am responsible for the selection, but for nothing more' (23 June 1884). But Algernon, who had read many of Waymark's opinions expressed in nearly the same language in Gissing's own letters, must have wondered at his brother's capacity for self-deception.

The effects of Gissing's division of mind may be illustrated by the comparatively strong novel, *Demos*, in which artistic and didactic elements are both present in well-developed form. It is concerned with the expression of two social theses: it condemns socialism on the ground that the lower classes are not worthy of wielding the power it delivers to them; and it shows that the faults of character resulting from proletarian environment and inheritance are not easily eliminated by changes in social status. As usual, Gissing drew his subject matter from contemporary conditions. In 1880 English socialism was hardly more than an ideal which had been proven unworkable by the Christian Socialists, but by 1885, when *Demos* was begun, it had grown into an active and vigorous movement. The novel tells the story of a radical working man, Richard Mutimer, who, after unexpectedly inheriting a fortune, uses his money to establish a factory based on a set of socialist principles which mingle

Owenism and St. Simonianism. His new wealth and power accentuate the defects he brings from his working-class background. Egotism and ambition lead him to marry an upper-middle-class girl who does not love him, and to run for Parliament. Lacking the faculty of imagination which Shelley regarded as the seat of ethical feeling, he is indifferent to the suffering of others and, as a result, abandons the poor London girl to whom he has been engaged, and deals harshly with some of his workers. A moral crisis is reached when his wife, Adela, finds a lost will which deprives him of his inheritance. Mutimer's impulse is to destroy the will, but Adela will not agree to this deception. The socialist experiment is shut down, and the Mutimers go to London to live in relative poverty. A new socialist crusade is halted when one of Mutimer's associates dupes him, and he is killed by a stone thrown from a mob of his followers who have turned against him.

The development of Mutimer's character is given a central position in *Demos* because Gissing intended it as a commentary on the socialist principles he espouses. He set himself the task of translating the ideological lesson he had in mind into the language of the novel, the language of character, motivation and plot, by relating the ideas in question to the actions and experiences of appropriate characters. In Mutimer he sought to create a convincing, self-contained, recognizable individual whose choice of socialist principles was as much a matter of character as anything else about him. They are principles which correspond to his temperament, talents, and understanding. Thus, the trial of the man may be regarded as a trial of his opinions, the defects of the socialist may fairly be said to cast a reflection on socialism itself, and the exposition of the failings of human nature becomes a criticism of the doctrine founded upon the excellence of human nature.

But the translation of ideas into the terms of Mutimer's character and actions is only partly intelligible. Many of the man's attributes belong, it is true, to Gissing's conception of his revolutionary movement. He is demagogic, ambitious, determined, and intelligent, but lacking in imagination and sensitivity. When he stirs up a political meeting with his speeches, the application to socialism is clear. His cruelty to his fiancée and his workers embodies the ruthlessness of his political creed. Many more such examples might be cited of Gissing's success in uniting fictional and doctrinal points. But there are too many critical junctures where the doctrinal application is obscure, or absent altogether. Mutimer courts and marries Adela because his new wealth has given him a taste for refinement, he abuses her through jealousy, he makes an unsound investment of funds belonging to others through greed and ambition. Actions like these reveal character, they spin the wheels of the plot, they play a part in perennial human conflicts and situations; in short they serve fictional ends. But they shed no light on social problems. It appears that as his work on *Demos* progressed, Gissing grew more and more absorbed in his character's psychology, and the whole question of social reform becomes—with the exception of some exciting scenes towards the end—little more than a topic of conversation. In fact, there are signs near the end of the novel that Mutimer's character is about to reform itself in a way which would compromise Gissing's social thesis. The socialist begins to regret many of his actions, and he and his wife draw somewhat closer together. A visit to his old mother's home arouses nostalgic memories of his youth, and makes him realize that he has lost sight of his original ideals. He seems to take on a life of his own, and is ready to lead the story into a course of events completely at odds with the lesson Gissing has in mind. In this way the ideological orientation of the story is subtly replaced by an interest closely related to the traditional artistic rôle of the novel, the study of character.

Character is, in fact, the standard by which Gissing chooses to judge socialism. The two sides of the question are represented by Mutimer and by Hubert Eldon, a young man of fanatically Conservative convictions. By making Mutimer self-seeking and hypocritical, Gissing gains the effect of undermining the ideals he advocates, no matter how admirable they may be in themselves. And by making Eldon a sincere though troubled man of firm principles, he wins a measure of respect even for his most inhuman attitudes. 'The difference between truth and cant often lies only in the lips that give forth the words,' says Gissing, commenting on a speech of Mutimer's (p. 377). To the extent that *Demos* judges its central problem by the standards of character rather than those of social justice it abandons its mission as a *roman à thèse* and assumes the qualities of an independent work of art.

Like *Demos* and *The Unclassed*, most of Gissing's novels violate those canons of 'A Defence of Poetry' which Gissing had adopted as his own in theory. *Workers in the Dawn* and *The Nether World* are concerned primarily, though by no means exclusively, with exposing the evils of poverty; *The Emancipated* and *The Odd Women* (1893) demonstrate the harm caused by the inferior social status of women;

New Grub Street (1891), *In the Year of Jubilee* and *The Crown of Life* (1899) attack puffery and commercialism; and so on. Although the influence of Shelleyan doctrines was usually enough to keep Gissing from framing his story as a clear illustration of a moral lesson, his strong opinions intruded in other ways. Throughout the vivid experiences of life which the novels offer, the reader is aware of the author at his shoulder, pointing to one detail after another as illustrations of an implicit lesson. Gissing's views can be recognized in the passages of comment which frequently occur, and felt in the tone of his language and his choice of vocabulary. Descriptions of the slums contain a note of outraged protest or deep sorrow; accounts of the bestial poor who inhabit them are alternately ironic and sympathetic. Politicians, socialists, and men of business are treated with varying degrees of contempt, but students and artists, no matter how lowly, meet with affection and respect. Significantly, when Gissing tried, as he did several times, to write a novel free of social preoccupations, the results were, except in a single case, failures. His one successful non-social novel was the historical romance, *Veranilda* (1904), and here it was his love for classical antiquity, another interest extraneous to the art of fiction, that motivated him.

It is difficult to escape the conclusion that Gissing, in spite of his professed 'worship' of 'pure art' was moved to exert his best powers, not by creation for its own sake, but by the hope of accomplishing a moral mission through his novels. He regarded realistic composition as an act of morality in itself, and he tried to make each novel an exercise in exact, unmitigated truth. In addition, he longed to pierce the complacency of the middle class, to punish prudery and hypocrisy with contemptuous irony, to startle a prosperous empire by revealing the horrible depths of suffering it sheltered, and shear it of its pride by exposing the baseness of its commercial ideals. But his devotion to the doctrines of 'A Defence of Poetry' made it impossible to think of motives like these as suitable ones for art, and led him to deny that the emotions aroused in him by social disorder had any claim upon him. His feeling of moral responsibility was no less profound than his artistic instinct; it was an energizing force which moved him to write, and played a vital part in the genesis and development of nearly all his novels. His most natural, most simple response to the experience that life had allotted to him was *saeva indignatio*. To write without that, as he learned from dashing off a few books that later haunted his conscience, was hardly to write at all. But his belief that art and social purpose were incompatible prevented him from realizing that as an artist who rebelled powerfully against social injustice his peculiar and necessary task was that of combining aesthetic and moral aims into a single harmonious whole.

PART TWO

Special Influences

8

*Influence of the Classics on Gissing's Novels of Modern Life**

SAMUEL VOGT GAPP

IT remains to draw certain generalizations from the material about Gissing's classic studies which has been presented in the preceding chapters. We shall discuss the influence of the classic on his novels of contemporary life, his appreciative and critical reaction to the classic literature, and his philosophy of culture, that is, his view of the place of classic studies in modern life. In considering the influence of the classic on his novels it will be well to limit the discussion to the typical Gissing slum novels. Such novels as *The Emancipated* and *Sleeping Fires* really need not come into consideration; the one is laid largely in Italy, the other largely in Greece; both are naturally full of classic references and could hardly have been written by any but a classicist. Many of his later novels hardly require treatment; they were mere potboilers, consciously written as works of light fiction. *New Grub Street* is another novel in which the influence of his classic studies is very evident; that fact is too familiar to require elaboration; besides, a novel whose characters are almost exclusively literary men is no true slum novel. As a realistic novelist Gissing is best remembered by *Thyrza, Demos*, and *The Nether World*, the works of his middle period. We will then consider the influence of classicism on his novels by a special study of *Demos* and *The Nether World*, drawing illustrations from the other works when necessary.

The most obvious case of classic influence on Gissing's novels is that of the direct or indirect use of classic reference. It is a fixed feature of his style, present in the slum novels no less than in those other works where it might be expected. In these novels it appears

* Reprinted by permission of the University of Pennsylvania Press from Samuel Vogt Gapp, *George Gissing, Classicist*, 1936, pp. 158-177.

most often on the part of the author; one could not expect the characters of such works to know their Latin or their Greek. Most often, I believe, he uses the classic by way of descriptive simile—as, for example, in his descriptions of a man's hat as in form 'exactly that of the old petasus', of Clem Peckover's shoulders as spreading 'like those of a caryatid', of her cruel lips as resembling those 'on certain fine antique busts'.[1] When he wants to say that a woman is beautiful, he says that she has 'features of the purest Greek type'; when he wants to say that a man is noisy, he speaks of the 'stentor-note of Daniel'.[2] Another man might have said 'stentorian'—hardly 'stentor-note'. The twelfth chapter of *The Nether World*, of course, is full of such similes and metaphors; we need only cite his ironic description of Clem as sweeping on 'like a stately ship of Tarsus, bound for the isles of Javan or Gadire'. A good example of his use of classic metaphor occurs later in the same book where he calls Clerkenwell Green 'that modern Agora'; earlier he had said of a beer-shop that 'through it ran a beery Pactolus'.[3] Such similes and metaphors are a regular part of his descriptive apparatus, especially in the earlier novels. Latin words or phrases, too, are used more frequently than one would expect; we encounter *impransus, ad libitum, sic voleo, sic jubeo, imprimatur, pia mater,* and many others. Now and then we come upon a kind of classic reference that is indeed rare in the English novel—a Greek word, deliberately transliterated into English and used in its Greek meaning. This is not so striking when a character like Reardon says: 'I haven't that diathesis'; he and Biffen were just the men who would throw in a Greek word now and then. It is more marked on the part of the author of a slum novel who says that an agitator 'would have found euthanasia'; it is most marked when he speaks of Rodman's schemes as 'a mere parergon'.[4] And, of course, the very title of *Demos* might be cited in this connection. The word appears frequently throughout the book; Mutimer is never a demagogue; he is simply demos—demos in the Greek sense, a member of the common people who has tried to step beyond the bounds fixed by fate for a man of his class. The word is also applied to the mob of workingmen which he leads in an exactly similar connotation; it is the demos of Plato, not the proletariat of the modern city, that rules the plot of this book.

[1] *The Nether World*, New York, n. d. (Dutton), pp. 1, 120, 8.
[2] *Demos*, New York, n. d. (Dutton), pp. 56, 60.
[3] *The Nether World*, pp. 181, 42.
[4] *New Grub Street*, p. 390. *Demos*, pp. 36, 305.

Such a use of classic reference may lay the author open to criticism. It certainly does not make for ease and lightness of style. Readers of the working class would hardly have appreciated such evidences of learning. But Gissing was not writing for such people; he would undoubtedly have classed them scornfully with the 'quarter-educated'. He was not writing with the hope that the proletariat would read his works. He may have thought of appealing to men of culture and refinement on their behalf, if indeed he would have allowed that his books had any ulterior, non-artistic purpose. Gissing would probably have felt that he was deliberately falsifying himself by 'writing down' to a lower level, had he omitted such references.

After all, they came naturally to him; they were part of his normal way of talking and writing. Few of them can be classed as purposeless; even the Greek words are used because they were the best way of expressing his meaning. Many of his more extended classic references are placed in the mouth of a character, and here they can hardly be criticized. Gissing does not make a worker quote Plato; it is but natural that Parson Wyvern should do so. Reardon and Biffen are exactly the men who would spend evenings discussing the Fragments of Euripides. Gissing's characters are often people who naturally have an interest in the classics.

A more important, if less obvious, influence of his studies is to be found in his characterization. The characters of his novels were, of course, largely the result of his observation of the people he met—but this statement is not true of Gissing to the extent to which it would be true of most novelists. In fact it is often asserted, and with much justice, that his characters are too often evolved from his own consciousness, or that they are mere transcripts of himself—examples of how George Gissing would have behaved in certain circumstances. What many critics are apt to forget is that these characters are the result of an adherence to a definite principle of selection. Gissing's learning was absolutely determinant in his choice of the type of character to be represented. If there is any one theme that is particularly his, it is that of the cultured man, of fine sensibilities and high literary ideals, at odds with the economic forces of the modern world. In his slum novels the slum-dwellers merely form the background for the poor scholar, unable to reconcile his ideal of the world as he has obtained it from books with that which goes on around him. Surely this is a direct heritage of the classic, that is, the theoretical, academic, non-practical type of mind which his early studies had implanted in him. He was conscious that this was his theme; in a letter to Roberts he wrote on 10 February 1895:

> My books deal with people of many social strata. . . . But what I desire to insist upon is this; that the most characteristic, the most important part of my work is that which deals with a class of young men distinctive of our time—well educated, fairly bred, but without money.[5]

This of course is the very theme of *New Grub Street*. Biffen and Reardon are devoted to the classics, and hopelessly poor. Their learning is the very cause of their failure; it has become an end in itself, not a means to economic success, as it was in the case of Milvain. The book is filled with learned characters; hardly a man of them but has pretensions to scholarship—and few enough are those who succeed in making a living through their learning. Even the genial Whelpdale supports himself only by playing up to the quarter-educated.

The best novels of Gissing, then, are studies of the impact of the modern world on the cultured student, as has been said in this discussion, I believe, almost too often. Sometimes the learned characters appear as the mouthpiece of their author; more often they are the protagonists of the action. In both cases they are the results of Gissing's studies in books. Wyvern is of course the best example of the Greek student as a mouthpiece. He expresses Gissing's own views about industrialism, about social reform, about marriage, about socialism, about education. There are many such characters. Some of them are content to be rather than to speak. Morton in *The Whirlpool* is an example of such a 'normal' character. It is interesting to note that Morton, as well as many other Gissing characters who fall under this classification, has, after all, the last word. A study of Gissing's last chapters would bring many similar cases to light, but this last chapter, in which Morton places his absorption in classic studies over against the active life which Kipling celebrates, is particularly important. Decius, too, in *Veranilda*, is a kind of mouthpiece, though his message is a negative one. He represents the viewpoint that, in such an age as that of the fall of Rome, there remains little but mere resignation and absorption in the past by way of literary and historical study. Mallard, in *The Emancipated*, is another such normal character, as are the Newthorpes in *Thyrza*. It is left to Earwaker in *Born in Exile* to represent the practical man of letters who succeeds without compromise, in sharp contrast to Milvain, who was, after all,

[5] *Virginia Quarterly Review*, July 1931, pp. 417-418.

a mere charlatan. It is Earwaker who pronounces the last verdict over the career of Peak; his words serve as an obituary for the unfortunate hero. Of course, Henry Ryecroft is the mouthpiece par excellence. Most of the time he is Gissing himself talking. His lonely life, his non-social outlook, his absorption in books, his philosophical bent, particularly the views he had arrived at by 1900—all are represented in the essays of Ryecroft.

The cultured hero as protagonist is, however, the typical Gissing character. His want of success in the struggle for existence is almost without exception. This usually results from his over-sensitiveness, his lack of social background, the fact that his intellectual approach to life is not shared by the people he meets, particularly the women, his inability to cope with the practical difficulties and small irritations of existence, his unwillingness to compromise with ideals that are not realizable in the conditions of modern life and the consequent poverty. It is a formidable list of disqualifications which the scholar, as Gissing conceived him, had to face. Biffen and Reardon, Milvain and Godwin Peak are examples of this type of character; all of them are really failures, for Milvain attains success only by the most shameless prostitution of his abilities. Egremont, in *Thyrza*, is perhaps the best case of the learned character as protagonist, for his work was directly in the sphere of culture. This young student, full of social enthusiasm, tries to reach the working classes intellectually and culturally—and his failure is total. He helps none of the workers except Gilbert Grail, a man who never had been representative of his class. Into this man's life he brings tragedy by depriving him of the wife he should have had. In fact, Egremont merely upsets things for all the working people he meets. Egremont, better than any other Gissing character, expresses the futility of the older learning in the face of modern social and intellectual conditions.

These characters stand in sharp contrast to the many ignoble and uncultured members of the proletariat who form the background for the man of culture and so frequently bring his work to failure. It may be said that Gissing overdoes this; that his poor and uncultured characters are generally mean, selfish, and grasping, utterly without any better self to which one might appeal. Characters like 'Arry Mutimer, Harriet Smales, Bob Hewett, and Clem Peckover have, indeed, little or no good about them. Gissing deliberately makes many of his poor people almost beyond hope of improvement. We need only quote his apostrophe to the charitably inclined ladies who fed the inhabitants of Shooter's Gardens:

> Gratitude, mesdames? You have entered upon this work with expectation of gratitude? And can you not perceive that these people of Shooter's Gardens are poor, besotted, disease-struck creatures of whom —in the mass— scarcely a human quality is to be expected?[6]

Such was his opinion of the inhabitants of the nether world, and his opinion of those of a higher station who remained still uneducated and uncultured was not a great deal better. Of course, when one considers them thoughtfully, Dickens' people are just as ignoble, but he has surrounded them with humour, with sentiment, with sympathy of various sorts; one feels that their distorted lives are the fault of the social order, not their own. There is no such relieving element in Gissing; he traces their faults directly to their inherent lack of the finer qualities of mind and character. Certainly this great group of characters forms a sharp contrast to those few well-educated men of fine sensibilities who are protagonists of the action. Gissing's learning, therefore, particularly his study of the seemingly refined society of ancient times, is largely responsible for his characterization. It was absolutely determinant in his choice of the characters who bear the brunt of the argument.

Another very definite trace of his classic studies appears in the setting of his various works. It is not merely that he so often describes places in figurative language which is drawn from his classic studies. The very spirit with which he approaches his description shows the classic student. This is true both negatively and positively. His slum description is on the negative side; it shows his adverse reaction to such scenes as he approaches them from his imaginings of the classic scene. His nature description is on the positive side. It is often in the classic mode; it is an attempt to transfer to the English countryside feelings and categories of thought which seem to have come to him from the *Georgics*. In brief, he does his descriptions of London by antipathy, and his nature descriptions in the tone of the classic idyllic poets. It is a familiar fact that many of his best descriptions are actuated by dislike. Morley Roberts has given us his memories of Gissing's experience in writing the Crystal Palace chapter in *The Nether World*. He states that Gissing spent a bank holiday there for the express purpose of writing this chapter and arrived home tired, worn out, and utterly disgusted with all that he had seen: 'It was with difficulty that I could imagine him sitting it out, even with the purpose that took him there. He spoke of the scene with bitterest disgust. This—this was humanity.'[7] The chapter cer-

[6] *The Nether World*, p. 252. [7] *The Nether World*, p. viii.

tainly bears out these statements; it is full of vivid details, of exact observations; it bears all the marks of a description written on the spot or from very recent memory; it concludes with the bitter comment: 'Since man came into being did the world ever exhibit a sadder spectacle?' The whole tone of the description is lugubrious, if not distinctly condemnatory. That kind of description is common in Gissing's slum novels. There is much of it in *Workers in the Dawn*; it is vividly exemplified in the description of Litany Lane in *The Unclassed*; *The Nether World* is full of it; one need only think of the several descriptions of Shooter's Gardens. One of the most characteristic examples of such a description is found in the first two pages of this same novel, pages which have often seemed to me among the best that Gissing ever wrote. Here there is no denunciation and the tone is quiet, but the piling on of detail after detail has a force that a more directly expressed dislike for the scene could never have had. This is the scene as Michael Snowdon passes a graveyard near the Middlesex House of Detention:

> At this corner the east wind blew with a malice such as it never puts forth save where there are poorly clad people to be pierced; it swept before it thin clouds of unsavoury dust, mingled with the light refuse of the streets. Above the shapeless houses night was signalling a murky approach; the sky—if sky it could be called—gave threatening of sleet, perchance of snow. And on every side was the rumble of traffic, the voiceful evidence of toil and of poverty; hawkers were crying their goods; the inevitable organ was clanging before a public-house hard by; the crumpet-man was hastening along, with monotonous ringing of his bell and hoarse rhythmic wail.

After reading such a description one can easily understand why the first two pages of *The Nether World* conclude with the statement that 'Something more than pain came over the old man's face as he looked and pondered'. The London of Gissing's early novels is, indeed, a city of dreadful night; it is only too often the home of the damned, as Mad Jack was wont to proclaim it in Shooter's Gardens. If London is not the scene of the bitterest struggles for existence, as it is in the slum novels, it is generally a drab, colourless place, full of endless streets whose small, poorly built and poorly furnished houses huddle up to the paved streets, leaving their unfortunate inhabitants literally no place to go by way of relief from the unhappy scene, and leaving them, of course, no opportunity at all to see anything that has the qualities of distinction or of beauty. One is reminded of the description of the two sections of Hoxton in the third chapter of *Demos*—the slums and the homes of the moderately well-paid workmen. 'The change,' says Gissing, 'is from undisguised struggle for subsistence to mean and spirit-broken leisure; hither retreat the better paid of the great slave-army when they are free to eat and sleep.' Such descriptions, of course, are a direct reflection of the author's early days in London. One can understand them best after reading some such essay as Spring X, in which Henry Ryecroft reviews his early days in London. 'Would I live it over again, that life of the garret and the cellar? Not with the assurance of fifty years' contentment such as I now enjoy to follow upon it!' We must remember that Gissing came to just such scenes only two short years after the conclusion of his school career, that happy time when he had been free to pursue his classic studies with his whole heart. It was the young classicist who lived amidst such surroundings, while his mind was still busy with the enchanted sea of the *Odyssey*, with the pastoral scenes of Virgil, with the countryside of Theocritus, with the Arcadian woods, still peopled by fauns and satyrs. It is not hard to explain his dislike of the London locale. It was the natural result of the impingement of a somewhat grimy reality on a mind full of imaginings of a far distant past as it presented itself—much glorified and brightened, no doubt—in its literature.

Less need be said about his descriptions of nature; it is obvious that much of it is the work of a classicist. His nature descriptions are remarkable above all for their sense of colour, but also for their careful observation of the smaller features of the landscape—of brooks, of trees, of birds and flowers, for the finely polished style he uses in them, and for the mood of quiet happiness, at times rising to ecstasy, with which he contemplates nature. The description of the orange trees at Catanzaro in the ninth chapter of *By the Ionian Sea* is typical of Gissing's best work of this type. It is occupied largely with colour—with the gold of the oranges contrasting with the deep green of the foliage, with the 'magic sea, purple and crimson as the sun descended', with the full moon rising over the mountains, a pale yellow moon against a 'sky soft-flushed with rose'. It closes with a reference to the garden of the Hesperides. Such descriptions appeared early in his career; the scene at the end of the seventeenth chapter of *The Unclassed* is a similar case. I much suspect, by the way, that this is all that is left of a scene which Gissing abbreviated greatly at the request of George Meredith;[8] evidently the description

[8] *The Private Life of Henry Maitland*, p. 161, and Gissing's *Letters*, p. 342.

of the younger man seemed too luxuriant, too colourful, perhaps too weighted down with classical fancies, to suit the reader for Chapman. The description of the Athenian sunset in *New Grub Street* is also a remarkably colourful bit. In reading such passages one is reminded over and over again of his love for the classic countries and for the classic pastoral and idyllic writers. Sometimes both of these types of description occur in close connection. The outstanding example of such a contrast comes in the nineteenth chapter of *The Nether World* where he is describing an excursion from London to the country.

> Over the pest-stricken regions of East London, sweltering in sunshine which served only to reveal the intimacies of abomination; across miles of a city of the damned, such as thought never conceived before this age of ours; above streets swarming with a nameless populace, cruelly exposed by the unwonted light of heaven; stopping at stations which it crushes the heart to think should be the destination of any mortal; the train made its way at length beyond the uttermost limits of dread, and entered upon a land of level meadows, of hedges and trees, of crops and cattle.

A short paragraph later we read:

> It is merely one of those quiet corners of flat, homely England, where man and beast seem on good terms with each other, where all green things grow in abundance, where from of old tilth and pastureland are humbly observant of seasons and alternations, where the brown roads are familiar only with the tread of the labourer, with the light wheel of the farmer's gig, or the rumbling of the solid wain. By the roadside you pass occasionally a mantled pool, where perchance ducks or geese are enjoying themselves; and at times there is a pleasant glimpse of farmyard, with stacks and barns and stables.

The contrast between Gissing's feeling about London and his feeling about the English countryside could hardly be more clearly expressed.

Both these types of description, then, are derived, for their spirit at least, and to a great extent even for their form, from Gissing's classic studies. It is interesting to note that Gissing was criticized for this very thing by no less prominent a nature writer than W. H. Hudson. Speaking of another writer altogether he wrote in a letter: 'Like Gissing, he is incapable of understanding or believing in a mind that can do with nature pure and simple and find it sufficient for happiness—very pleased to let all books . . . go hang.'[9] Hudson

[9] W. H. Hudson, *Men, Books, and Birds*, London, 1925, p. 189.

correctly states Gissing's attitude towards nature, the attitude of a man who does not take it 'pure and simple', as Hudson did, but who sees it through literary spectacles—spectacles, in Gissing's case, which had been made by his early reading of the classics. Gissing and Hudson knew each other; it might be possible to make an interesting comparison of their differing descriptive styles, but that is impossible here. At any rate, it is precisely in the settings of his novels and of his semi-narrative essays alike that Gissing seems to have done his best work. He had a good faculty of observation and he was deeply affected by his surroundings, whether by way of joy or by way of disgust. His descriptions give the impression of reality, of sincerity, of a force of feeling. Here is a part of his novels which he felt and felt deeply. It is the sort of thing which a non-social being could do, could attain mastery in, as such a person could not do in the analysis of character and situation. The classic background of this phase of his work should not be forgotten.

It is rather difficult to say much about the influence of Gissing's classic studies upon his style without merely being vague. It is present, though, and none the less important because it is intangible. His style is evidently that of a student. It is somewhat formal; in his earlier books it is even ornate, rather loaded down with classic references and full of difficult and unusual words. It is quiet and subdued, seldom robust, vigorous, or forceful except when he is expressing a dislike for something. The descriptive and reflective parts rather over-balance the action, and Gissing is too fond of a rather irritating apostrophe to the reader. The most classic feature of his style is probably its carefulness, its attention to the rhythm of the sentence. One is reminded of Biffen's efforts in finishing 'Mr. Bailey, Grocer': 'He had laboured over it for many months, patiently, affectionately, scrupulously. Each sentence was as good as he could make it, harmonious to the ear, with words of precious meaning skilfully set.'[10] This kind of work was his ideal and he did attain it frequently. It is certainly in his sentence construction, in the details of the work, and not in the organization of the work as a whole or in the technique of the novel, that we are to look for traces of any classic influence. Gissing's later style is familiar enough to the average reader, but an example of his earlier style might be of interest. The beginning of the twenty-eighth chapter of *The Nether World* is representative.

[10] *New Grub Street*, p. 456.

> With the first breath of winter there passes a voice half-menacing, half-mournful, through all the barren ways and phantom-haunted refuges of the nether world. Too quickly has vanished the brief season when the sky is clement, when a little food suffices, and the chances of earning that little are more numerous than at other times; this wind that gives utterance to its familiar warning is the vaunt-courier of cold and hunger and solicitude that knows not sleep. Will the winter be a hard one? It is the question that concerns this world before all others, that occupies alike the patient workfolk who have yet their home unbroken, the strugglers foredoomed to loss of such scant needments as the summer gifted them withal, the hopeless and the self-abandoned and the lurking creatures of prey. To all of them the first chill breath from a lowering sky has its voice of admonition; they set their faces; they sigh, or whisper a prayer, or fling out a curse, each according to his nature.

Most of the typical Gissing style is there—the careful, well-rounded, thoughtful sentences, the unusual compound words, the preponderance of Latin derivatives, the coined word like 'needments', the really remarkable slow and sad rhythm.

The most evident stylistic trace of his classic studies is his diction. Even in writing of the most uncultured of men he uses the diction of the scholar. These unusual, Latinate words are used so often, in fact, that he sometimes seems pedantic. At times this is deliberately done; when Gissing chooses to be sarcastic, one can always expect words which smell of the dictionary. Hell appears as 'a certain igneous realm'; 'that aristocratic vacuity of visage' is attributed to 'carefully induced cerebral atrophy'; Mutimer's table manners are indicated by the fact that he has just discovered that 'manducation and absorption of fluids must be performed without audible gusto'.[11] Mustard appears as 'condiment', grease as 'oleaginous matter'; Clem Peckover uses 'the vituperative vernacular of the nether world'.[12] Well, it is but a schoolmaster's idea of humour. But this kind of diction is common throughout his works. 'Leafage', 'verdure', 'tillage', 'vale', and other similar words occur in the space of two sentences. Mr. Wyvern's clerical clothes are described as 'sable garniture'; his 'towering sableness' is mentioned; 'unflinching orbs' is used instead of 'steady eyes'; when Adela blushes, 'the subsiding warmth left a pearly translucency as of a lily petal against the light'; the author speaks of the soul's 'hidden velleities', of 'supernal spheres'.[13] This

[11] *Demos*, pp. 1, 33, 89.
[12] *The Nether World*, pp. 6, 8, 158.
[13] *Demos*, pp. 3, 4, 10, 80, 333, 416.

kind of diction is obviously a direct heritage of his classic studies. In his later works his language becomes simpler, freer from unusual or coined words, not so studded with Latin and Greek derivatives and is all the better for it.

The most important influence of the classics upon his novels is in the realm of ideas. His classic studies have lent to the novels their tone and their point of view. I refer, of course, to the aristocratic point of view, to the ideals of gentility, of bookish leisure, of withdrawal from the everyday world which form so obvious an anomaly in works whose material is drawn from the poorest classes of society. Gissing is no true novelist of revolt; he speaks often as a conservative country squire might speak. This is a direct heritage of his classic study. It is a familiar fact that the classic literature was an aristocratic one. It took little account of slaves, of poor artisans, of the hordes of freemen who filled the Circus Maximus in the Rome of the Caesars. It was a literature written by men who reclined at ease in their villas. It was often definitely the product of an imperial court, as in the Augustan age. Proletarian literature was simply inconceivable in ancient times. In the education of modern times the classic literatures have found a similar and appropriate destiny. They are not taught to artisans; a classic education is synonymous with a professional training; it is the privilege of the professional classes, of lawyers, doctors, divines, of the wealthy classes, or of statesmen. Naturally, then, classic training produces a conservative attitude of mind. Gissing shared to the full such ideals and never, as far as I can make out, deserted them, although he had every excuse to do so. He may have detested the conventions of morals, society's set of values; he did not question the right of established society to be what it was, nor did he believe that much good would come from its overthrow. It is needless to repeat that he had no faith in the lower orders of society. *Demos* amounts to an attack on socialism, upon democracy, upon popular education, upon the fitness of the masses to be masters of their own destiny. Its hero, Richard Mutimer, is meant to be representative of the better type of working-man. Gissing tries hard to be fair to him, but Mutimer is a sorry sham, for all that. His ideas for the betterment of the lot of the worker are founded on ignorance, egotism, and a desire for personal renown. He basely deserts the girl he was engaged to, and marries a lady. He dishonestly plans to conceal a will. He refuses to know his old friends after he has risen in the world. His own mother regards him as a mere talker. His companions are little better; their interest in socialism never rises higher than that of Daniel Dabbs to whom economic agitation was a 'mode of passing a few hours amid congenial uproar'. Their meetings are a farce, utterly lost to reason and common sense. There is, in fact, 'a monstrous gulf between men of that kind and cultured human beings'. The city mob which Mutimer leads is formed of 'the enemies of every man who speaks the pure English tongue and does not earn a living with his hands'.[14] Gissing's poor people. in this book at least, resemble no other historical group so much as the mobs of the French Revolution. Individually, they may be people of some value; collectively, they are the enemies of all that is good in civilization.

Such being his view of the proletariat, it is easy to see that Gissing held out no hope for any real improvement in their condition; any effort to improve their situation which did not involve an improvement of their mass character he regarded as futile. *Demos* inveighs against the folly of leaving money to a representative of this class. Richard Mutimer's uncle did not intend to leave him the money. 'To leave wealth to young men of the working-class would have seemed to him the most inexcusable of follies; if such were to rise at all, it must be by their own efforts and in consequence of their native merits.'[15] Nevertheless, Richard Mutimer does obtain the money, with consequences disastrous to himself and all which is his. Mutimer's own character is degraded, and he comes to his death; his brother becomes a loafer and a drunkard; his sister bigamously marries an adventurer; the poor workers are in the end worse off than they had been before he started to help them. To give the poor money was no solution in Gissing's mind. He goes even further than that; he denies that much good can come of educating the average poor man. He feels that the average man of such classes lacks the capacity for education and will use his knowledge to the general harm of all. The plight of a man educated beyond his social and economic station is another one of his recurring themes. Mr. Wyvern has this to say about it:

> Take one feature of it—universal education. That, I believe, works most patently for the growing misery I speak of. . . . It is a class created by the mania of education, and it consists of those unhappy men and women whom unspeakable cruelty endows with intellectual needs whilst refusing them the sustenance they are taught to crave.[16]

[14] *Demos*. pp. 35, 383, 376. [15] *Ibid*., p. 29. [16] *Ibid*., p. 384.

This, I presume, was Gissing's own view with respect to the classical and cultural education as imposed on the lower classes. He thought no better of what might be called a practical education—witness his description of Mutimer's library. Education is simply an injury to those who are incapable of a cultured and refined outlook on life. Social and economic agitation, too, is a futile way of trying to improve the condition of the poor. English socialism, says Eldon, is 'infused with the spirit of shop-keeping; it appeals to the vulgarest minds; it keeps one eye on personal safety, the other on the capitalist's strong-box'. Mr. Wyvern will have nothing to do with it and informs his parishioners: 'I am a Christian, madam, and have nothing to do with economic doctrines.'[17] Certainly the pictures of various types of socialists—the well-intentioned but ignorant Mutimer, the violently denunciatory Roodhouse, the scholarly, refined, and purely theoretical Westlake—would not dispose the readers of *Demos* to think well of the movement. It is not that Gissing has simply adopted a capitalistic viewpoint from his education; his condemnation of the selfishly wealthy classes is as violent as his condemnation of the agitators. He simply believes that the masses are at present unfit for any position except the one they now hold, and that no good can come of a change in the social order unless the masses can be improved culturally, intellectually, and morally. Social agitation offends, in his view, against the very spirit of culture. One remembers the protest he made against the part William Morris took in revolutionary movements; in *Demos* he says that such agitation has even caused Westlake's style to deteriorate: 'His very style has abandoned him, his English smacks of the street corners, of Radical clubs.'[18] In fact, Gissing is generally committed to the position that a poor man, of the lower social order, can improve his position only with difficulty. The outstanding case in his novels is that of Godwin Peak in *Born in Exile*. Here we have an individual, not a group, and a man of pronounced talents and considerable ability. He aims, as a plebeian, to marry a lady. His efforts result only in putting himself in an entirely false position where his very sincerity can be questioned. His aims, like Gissing's own, were derived from a cultural education, but he simply was on the wrong track. He had overstepped the bounds allotted by fate and attempted that which the decrees of the immortal gods had forbidden.

Such views naturally imply a great deal of respect for the ideals associated with the word 'gentleman' and a belief in the reality of

[17] *Ibid.*, pp. 381-382, 87.

[18] *Demos*, p. 381.

class distinction. Gissing had both the respect and the belief. A gentleman, to him, was a person of education and culture, a man of refined sensibilities with a broad, liberal, but realistic outlook on life, one possessed of those very social graces which he himself did not always possess. Even that old plebeian, the elder Mutimer, appreciated such ideals. He sought money only as a means; '. . . the end he really aimed at being the satisfaction of instincts which could only have play in a higher social sphere'. 'He bowed in sincere humility to those very claims which the Radical most angrily disallows: birth, hereditary station, recognized gentility.' There is no better way of stating the difference between Eldon and Mutimer than to say that the one was, and the other was not, a gentleman. Even Mrs. Waltham, who has married her daughter to the wealthy plebeian, feels this. 'Oh, but Mr. Eldon is a gentleman—he can never exact his legal rights to the full extent. He has too much delicacy of feeling for that.'[19] Such are the grasping old lady's real views, despite her actions. The admission of such an ideal means that class distinctions are real and fairly permanent because they are based on realities, on real differences. Because of such realities Adela gradually loses her respect for her husband, the representative of Demos. This gradual loss of respect reaches its culmination as she watches his sleeping face in the railroad coach on the way back to London.

> Beholding that face as if it were that of a man unknown to her, she felt that a whole world of natural antipathies was between it and her.
>
> It was the face of a man by birth and breeding altogether beneath her. . . .
>
> Their life of union was a mockery; their married intimacy was an unnatural horror. He was not of her class, not of her world; only by violent wrenching of the laws of nature had they come together. She had spent years in trying to convince herself that there were no such distinctions, that only an unworthy prejudice parted class from class. One moment of true insight was worth more than all her theorizing on abstract principles. . . .[20]

Such is Gissing's general statement of the problem.

His opinion on such subjects remained unchanged; much the same philosophy appears in *The Private Papers of Henry Ryecroft*, published only two years before his death. Its very theme is that of a hack writer who by chance reaches the condition of a gentleman. In miniature, he is a member of the landed and moneyed gentry—a man of fine feelings who appreciates the simple comforts of life, the

[19] *Demos*, pp. 28, 328. [20] *Ibid.*, pp. 350-351.

beauty of nature, and the beauties of the great books of the world's literature. He is still against the demos of the city: Spring XVI, with its formidable opening sentence, 'I am no friend of the people', is enough to prove that. He is still against the quarter-educated, as his criticism of the periodical literature of his day in Spring XXII shows. He still believes in social differences; we all remember the unhappy fate of the young workingman who tried to eat in a restaurant frequented by people of a higher class than his own (Summer XVII). He is still unconvinced by the propaganda in favour of democracy (Summer XXII). Such ideas as these formed the most important part of all the influences on his novels which Gissing's classical education exerted. These ideas are characteristic of all his writing, and they are very closely connected with the studies in the classics begun in his youth and continued throughout his life. These studies were responsible for the one unique note of Gissing—the combination of slum material, sympathy for the sufferings of the lower classes, with a demand for culture, for the ideals of gentility, for an interest in strictly intellectual pursuits.

9

*Gissing, Turgenev and Dostoyevsky**

GILBERT PHELPS

AT first glance the suggestion that Turgenev was a powerful influence in the work of George Gissing appears almost ludicrous: his whole approach and method of composition, which strike us today as so characteristically English, seem utterly recalcitrant to it.

His interest in Russia itself is of course evident from his novels and particularly from *The Crown of Life* (1899), whose hero lives for many years in Russia and which has numerous references to Russian literature, politics and so on. We have Gissing's word for it too that the writers who were helping him most in his formative years were French and Russian, and his letters show that among these Russian writers Turgenev figured prominently. In 1883 for example he was writing to his sister Ellen, describing him as 'without doubt the greatest living writer of fiction': a year later he was 'very busy with Tourguéneff', reading 'five or six' of his novels in German. He was proud of the two letters which, he told Ellen, he had received from Turgenev 'on matters of business'—probably in connection with a proposal that he should write a series of articles on English literature for the St. Petersburg periodical the *Messager de l'Europe*, and in another of the letters he proclaimed 'he is a man I glory in'.

It is generally assumed, however, that whatever Russian influence there is in Gissing derives from Dostoyevsky, and as we shall see there is some justification for this view. Nevertheless Turgenev was for him too, in his most impressionable period, 'the novelists' novelist', and in some respects the influence of Dostoyevsky in his work has been exaggerated. Thus although his studies of 'minds maddened by hunger' (as he expressed it in the book on Dickens) are Dostoyev-

* Reprinted by permission of the Hutchinson Publishing Group Ltd. from Gilbert Phelps, *The Russian Novel in English Fiction*, London, 1956, pp. 88-94 and 163-164.

skyan in their intensity, his approach is on the whole closer to Turgenev's. It is ethical and moral rather than psychological or mystical: even in the so-called 'Dostoyevskyan' novels, such as *Workers in the Dawn* (1880), the main interest is concentrated on certain clear-cut moral problems which beset the characters, and as in Turgenev, the story is about the ways in which they resolve them. Character for both novelists is in fact the crux.

Gissing's portrayal of squalor and wretchedness, moreover, has no deep affinity with Dostoyevsky's. One of his main purposes, as he tells us himself, was to correct the over-optimistic picture presented by Dickens, and his Realism in this respect probably owes as much to Zola as it does to Dostoyevsky. He has had personal experience of poverty and suffering, and is in consequence able to communicate them faithfully, but his attitude towards them is often, particularly in the earlier books, one of resentment, open or concealed. He writes as a man who has been brought low by misfortune, but who feels himself fundamentally aloof from the environment into which it has forced him. The characters who engage his sympathy in his representations of slum life are those of 'superior' status—artisans or members of the lower-middle classes, who also feel aloof from their surroundings. Of the masses as such he is bitterly scornful, and there is in fact a good deal of misanthropy in his earlier work. He reveals little of Dostoyevsky's emotional and imaginative identification with poverty, suffering and evil, and his pity and understanding in consequence are nothing like as profound.

His favourite characters in fact are closer to the types portrayed by Turgenev than to the curious, fluid, paradoxical, shifting figures of Dostoyevsky. The typical heroes—Golding in *Workers in the Dawn*, Egremont in *Thyrza* (1887), Waymark in *The Unclassed* (1884), to some extent Piers Otway in *The Crown of Life*, bear a clearly recognizable relationship to Dmitri Rudin or Nezhdanov. They have the same highly strung temperaments, and the same instability of purpose, particularly in relation to marriage, and all of them compare, unfavourably, with their womenfolk. They are usually possessed, moreover, of some high moral purpose. Sometimes this takes the form of an ideal which the hero has set before him, and sometimes he succeeds in attaining, or maintaining, it—Piers Otway, for example, eventually achieves his 'crown of life' when he wins Irene's love. But often, as with Turgenev and James, the characters become 'morally interesting' only in failure. Thus Annabel says to Egremont after Thyrza's death:

'The crisis of your life was there. There was your great opportunity, and you let it pass. She could not have lived; but that is no matter. You were tried, Mr. Egremont, and found wanting.'

Egremont's betrayal of Thyrza, moreover, springs from the fundamental falsity of his position in relation to 'the people' in a way that vividly recalls Dmitri Rudin and Nezhdanov. Like them he is young, cultured, of superior birth and breeding, full of vague aspirations and yearnings, and vexed by a social conscience. Like them he is in revolt against the privileges and conventions of his class, and endeavours to find an outlet for his personal insecurities and dissatisfactions by 'going to the people'. Like them he remains, in spite of his sensitivity and the sincerity of his desire to serve, irrevocably of his own class, and his essential remoteness is thrown into relief by his association with genuine men of the people—thus Nezhdanov's relationship with Solomin is echoed by that of Egremont with Gilbert Grail, and in the event Egremont like Nezhdanov, though his solution is neither as drastic nor as heroic, runs away from his *impasse*.

There are of course vast differences in the environments and conditions against which the two novelists operate, but Egremont illustrates much the same sort of response to social change and the challenges that accompany it as do Rudin and Nezhdanov. Fundamentally there is here no difference between the Revolutionary and the Adult Education Lecturer.

This patterning in Gissing admittedly does not derive from Turgenev's influence alone. To some extent it is yet another instance of a certain similarity in social environments producing a certain similarity in fictional types. For Gissing too, as Morley Roberts pointed out in his Preface to the 1927 edition of *Thyrza*, was, like so many of his characters, a 'man of exile'; he was the product of a society in a state of flux, a man who felt himself without a real class of his own, or a real place in the social structure into which he was born. This is also of course a characteristic artist's predicament, one that besets many artists in many periods of civilization. In a sense the artist is always an exile, and this is perhaps one of the most important reasons why Turgenev, with his portraits of alienation which are almost universal prototypes, has become 'the novelists' novelist'.

Nevertheless it seems clear that in the writing of many of his novels Gissing was following Turgenev's example in a more straightforward sense. Egremont in *Thyrza* is not merely the repetition of a basic type, and indeed a specific hint that Gissing was thinking of Turgenev as he wrote is provided by Mr. Newthorpe's statement that he feels he is just the kind of character of whom Turgenev would have made 'an admirable study'. In *Isabel Clarendon* (1886) there are clues of a similar nature. For example, Thomas Meres urges Ada to read a novel by Turgenev in which he is confident she will 'rejoice'. This was probably *Fathers and Children*, and indeed there are recognizable echoes of Turgenev's novel to be found in Gissing's. Isabel's situation, for example, is similar to that of Anna Sergyevna ('how clearly I see Mme Odintsoff!' Gissing wrote to Ellen): she is not of course so much the *femme fatale*, she is warmer, and very English, with a good deal in common with some of Trollope's heroines, but in her weakness for society and for creature comforts even at the expense of integrity and of genuine passion, she reminds one of Bazarov's temptress, while her relationship to Ada recalls that of Anna Sergyevna to Katya. It is however in the portrayal of his curious, and not particularly likeable hero Kingcote, that the Russian influence is particularly apparent. It was of Kingcote, presumably, that Morley Roberts was thinking when, in his Preface to *Thyrza*, he wrote of *Isabel Clarendon* as above all revealing 'its Russian affinities and his own temperament, equally plainly akin to many of the Russian writers from Turgenev onward'.

Now we know from Gissing's letters that Bazarov made a powerful impression on him—'a wonderfully drawn character' he told Ellen when at last he had persuaded her to read *Fathers and Children*. And his description of him in the same letter as an example of 'the purely negative mind, common enough nowadays in men of thought' is certainly applicable to Kingcote. More appropriately indeed than to Bazarov himself who, after all, as a person is by no means 'purely negative', and whose Nihilism, unsatisfactory though it may be as a progressive doctrine of action, does not preclude hard work, and a belief both in Science and in himself. Kingcote is typical rather of the Western interpretation of the word 'Nihilism' (Gissing incidentally uses it in his letter to Ellen) and in his case it involves an almost complete abnegation of effort.

He is closer to Bazarov, however, in some of his nihilistic utterances, particularly in those calculated to 'shock the bourgeoisie'. He surprises Mrs. Stratton, for example, by agreeing with her, though with a passion she had hardly bargained for, about the exaggerated importance attached to Education, and in much the same way he pours scorn on all the other accepted traditions and conventions of society. Like Bazarov too he has no use for the 'sentimental' beliefs of Liberalism and he is as scathing as he is about the peasantry.

> At times I talk with a farm labourer . . . to do so I have to divest myself of the last rags of civilization, to strip my mind to its kernel. Were oxen suddenly endowed with speech they would utter themselves as these peasants do. . . .

Kingcote has little of Bazarov's inherent strength of character, and his negativism is personal and psychological rather than doctrinaire—Bazarov, for example, would have scorned Kingcote's misanthropy as itself a sentimental indulgence. At bottom in fact he is a Liberal idealist (of the type that Gissing was to portray a year later in Egremont) who has become so disillusioned that he speaks with the negativism of Bazarov, but with a personal bitterness that Bazarov does not possess. It is as if Arkady and Bazarov had somehow become merged into one and the mixture had turned sour.

Even for Gissing, moreover, unlikely though it may seem, Turgenev was 'the novelists' novelist' in a more narrowly technical sense. When in a letter of 1885 for example he criticizes the old-fashioned English three-decker novel, and states his belief in 'the later method of merely suggesting, of dealing with episodes, instead of writing biographies' as 'far more artistic', it is obvious that he is thinking of Turgenev, six of whose novels, as we have seen, he had bought in German translation the year before. He sounds, indeed, almost as if he had joined the Atlantic Monthly school when he goes on to deplore the old 'omniscient' novelist.

> 'I think it is better,' he writes, 'to tell a story precisely as one does in real life, hinting, surmising, telling in detail what can be told, and no more. In fact, it approximates to the dramatic mode of presentment.'

These are curious pronouncements coming from Gissing, whose novels seem so thoroughly English in their leisurely narration and looseness of structure—and indeed it was only a year later that *Isabel Clarendon* was published in two volumes. The novel is certainly the reverse of Turgenev's delicately moulded structures, but there is no doubt that Gissing, like so many other English novelists who themselves conspicuously lacked the Russian's qualities of grace and economy, set him up as his ideal. There are indeed signs in *Isabel Clarendon* of an attempt to put the precepts he had formulated in his letter into practice: much of the 'character analysis' of the hero, for example, which Gissing, in the traditional English way, would have normally conducted himself, is 'dramatically' communicated by Kingcote—often, it must be admitted, in long and clumsy speeches which merely sound like author's comment put in inverted commas.

. . . .

It was George Gissing who had first drawn attention to Dostoyevsky's humour in his book on Dickens, published in 1898. The passages where he compares Dostoyevsky and Dickens reveal an understanding of certain aspects of the Russian's work, and a depth of imaginative response to them, that are considerably in advance of his time. One of the major influences in Dostoyevsky's work was that of Dickens, and Gissing was the first to appreciate the basic similarities between the two writers. Dickens, he argued, but for the differences of race and upbringing, might well have written *Crime and Punishment*: the chapters dealing with Marmeledov's drunkenness and degradation were particularly Dickensian—and the elements of a plot involving murder, detection, a ruined girl who keeps her soul clean, a criminal redeemed by love, and faith in Christ, might well have appealed to Dickens.

What made Gissing important from the point of view of Dostoyevsky's future reputation however was his assertion that as a Realist Dostoyevsky was actually superior to Dickens—and his analysis of the fundamental reason. This, he argued, lay simply in the fact that Dostoyevsky was able to face facts which 'Dickens was obliged to ignore or to hint, with sighing timidity'. The character of Sonia, for example, was inconceivable in English fiction, and

> the crucial chapter . . . the magnificent scene in which Raskolnikov makes confession to Sonia, is beyond Dickens as we know him; it would not have been so but for the defects of education and the social prejudices which forbade his gifts to develop.

Raskolnikov too, Gissing argued—'his motives, his reasonings'—could not be comprehended by an Englishman of the middle class. As for the murder itself—Bill Sikes and Jonas Chuzzlewit

> show but feebly after we have watched that lank student with the hatchet under his coat, stealing up the stairs; when we have seen him do his deed of blood, and heard the sound of that awful bell tinkling in the still chamber.

Gissing therefore re-stated the moral challenge as far as Dostoyevsky's Realism was concerned, while his own imaginative nerves stirred in response to the Russian's narrative powers. There can be no doubt that the example of Sonia in *Crime and Punishment*, reinforced by the strange circumstances of his own life, encouraged him to depict 'fallen women' in such novels as *The Unclassed* (1884). As Morley Roberts suggested too, in his Preface to the 1927 edition of *Thyrza*, Gissing's sombre vision of poverty and slum life was clearly affected by his reading of Dostoyevsky.

It seems very probable too that in describing the more feverish states of mind of his heroes Gissing had the example of Raskolnikov in mind. Kingcote in *Isabel Clarendon*, for example, especially at the time of his illness, indulges in extremes of self-laceration that often strike one as decidedly 'un-English' in the context of a nineteenth-century novel, as one of the other characters, Robert Asquith, seems to feel—'Something morbid about him, I suppose,' he remarks to Isabel; 'he looks in fact rather bloodless, like a man with a fixed idea.'

Isabel Clarendon was published in 1886, and it seems likely that Dérély's *Le Crime et le Châtiment*, published two years previously, was among the translations of Russian books to which Gissing referred in the letter to his sister from which we have already quoted.

10

*Gissing and Schopenhauer**

C. J. Francis

I

Gissing did not very often call himself, unreservedly, a realist. He did once contrast the novelists of the school of Dickens with 'our school of strict veracity, of realism'.[1] In other places he implied his sympathy with the realists without directly committing himself.[2] In practice, of course, he belonged to the school of Dickens quite as much as to any school of 'strict veracity', and there are few of his novels that are not overtly formed in the manner of Dickens, in plot, character, situation, and construction. It is true, however, that he did attempt always to serve the ideals of impersonality, objectivity, and veracity; furthermore, he was influenced directly by his reading of French and Russian novelists, especially Zola and Turgenev. The resulting clash of incompatibles (he was quite right in considering the two schools to be opposites) causes his novels to resemble a literary battlefield; at times, the work of not one but two different writers. The detailed effects themselves form an intriguing study.

One is tempted to say that Gissing had very little idea of what he was doing when he wrote. True, his writings on Dickens show he had analytical ability; his habit of extensive rewriting would suggest that he had also the power of criticizing his own works. On the other hand, there is a certain paucity of critical comment in his various writings, especially in reference to his own novels. (Where personal letters are concerned, it may be unfair to think that reticence indi-

[1] *Charles Dickens, a Critical Study* (London, 1898), p. 90.

[2] 'The Place of Realism in Fiction,' *Selections Autobiographical and Imaginative* (London, 1929), p. 219; *Isabel Clarendon* (London, 1886), II, chap. vi and other places.

cates anything more than consideration for a non-literary correspondent; but it is at least noticeable that his comments on the novels he is writing are usually limited to estimates of the degree of completion or something equally noncommittal.) But by contrast there is this:

> My attitude henceforth is that of the artist pure and simple. The world is for me a collection of phenomena, which are to be studied and reproduced artistically. In the midst of the most serious complications of life, I find myself suddenly possessed with a great calm, withdrawn as it were from the immediate interests of the moment, and able to regard everything as a picture.[3]

This could be a direct statement of a plank in the realist's platform: the withdrawal of the artist from personal intervention, so far as it is possible, in the world which he represents, in the belief that he will thus be enabled to draw a truer picture of it. How was it possible, after so clear a statement (which can in fact be taken as a statement of his final position), that he so signally failed to achieve with any consistency either this impersonality or any other of the techniques of realism? I believe this is because he arrived at this statement not as a result of technical experiment, in which case his form and method must have reflected the opinion directly, but as a result of philosophical meditation. The quotation is immediately preceded by: 'I am by degrees getting my right place in the world. Philosophy has done all it can for me, and now scarcely interests me any more.'

I shall shortly explain this rejection of philosophy; I quote this here to show that he was at this time speaking rather about philosophy than art. In another letter shortly before he had said:

> I am growing to feel that the only thing known to us of absolute value is artistic perfection. The ravings of fanaticism—justifiable or not—pass away; but the works of the artist, work in what material he will, remain, sources of health to the world.[4]

Unoriginal though this may be, it is clearly a statement of abstract value. In this light, we can take his classification of himself as 'artist pure and simple' to be mainly a preference for a certain attitude to the living of life and not, as it first appears to be, a commendation of

[3] Letter to his brother, 18 July 1883, *Letters of George Gissing to Members of his Family* (London, 1927), p. 128.

[4] Letter, 12 May, 1883, *ibid.*, p. 126.

a certain creative method. The attitude implies the method, but Gissing's incomplete achievement of the method may indicate that he did not see the connection with absolute clarity.

Both these ideas, concerning the method and the value of art, are expressed by Schopenhauer, in his own terms and in relation to his own basic ideas. 'Objectivity alone makes one capable of being an artist,' he said.[5] Knowledge, when serving the Will, perceives only the relations of things, their use and purpose; this is subjectivity, implying the observer's active participation in what he is observing. If the observer is withdrawn from participation, his volitions are not involved, and Knowledge can clearly perceive the nature of the thing. (In Schopenhauer's terminology, the Idea of it.) To perceive a thing clearly, the observer must cease to be conscious of himself.

Like the realists, Schopenhauer conceives of art as an attempt to apprehend the essential Idea, to represent the Truth itself, to reproduce and clarify the thing outside the artist rather than his view of it. Subjective artists wish to convey their personal conception of life; the realists are aware that the artist's personal view must inevitably distort the things seen through him, but they consider this unfortunate and wish to suppress the personal element so far as possible. In consequence, they believe that the inclusion of opinions and recommendations in a novel is reprehensible. Schopenhauer was probably thinking on similar lines when he distinguished between philosophizing, the communication of abstract thinking about a subject, and art, which is the communication of the perception of a thing. He feels that art is better when it is limited to matters of perception only. Thus he arrives at the same position as the realist: impersonality and objectivity are essentially the proper creative method. He goes so far as to say that an absolute objective perception of some kind is the condition and germ of every work of art.

Like Gissing, he finds art, when thus detached from volition and opinion, of absolute value. In his view the suppression of the Will is to be commended, on moral grounds. The Ideas appeal more readily from art than from reality, because reality is closely related to our volitions, whereas the subject of a work of art is not; consequently, art encourages as well as expresses calm contemplation, the exercise of the faculty of Knowing without the Will.

[5] Haldane and Kemp (tr.), *The World as Will and Idea* (London, 1886, III, 135.

II

It is my belief that this parallel between Gissing's and Schopenhauer's views of art is not merely accidental; that Gissing arrived at these views under the direct influence of Schopenhauer, and that, as I have suggested already, the unevenness of his artistic method is the result of his being a theorist on speculative and not artistic matters. Specifically, I would suggest that he wrote, without thinking about it very clearly, in the manner of Dickens, in most of his books at least; but that the fact of his attempting also to maintain an objective attitude, so different from Dickens's, caused not only some very odd fluctuations of tone but also some interesting variations in form. There is no question of his slowly throwing off the influence of Dickens and substituting something else; this conflict between two methods he shows both early and late.

To follow up this critical theme by examination of the novels would require more than one article. Here I shall show that the association between Gissing and Schopenhauer is not one I have made arbitrarily; that the influence of Schopenhauer can be found in the novelist's content as well as his form. To do this, we must necessarily consider Morley Roberts's remark: 'From the day of his birth to the day of his death, he took no interest whatever in science and hated all forms of speculative thought'[6] (in this time of religious-scientific controversy, 'science' was almost a synonym for 'speculative thought'), and also Gissing's own statements in *The Private Papers of Henry Ryecroft* that he hated and was disturbed by science and particularly scientific speculation.[7] Neither of these half-fictional biographies of Gissing can wholly be trusted, because of the fictional aspect; furthermore, Gissing is expressing, in so far as he is expressing his own opinions, ideas of his middle age—and it was in his later years that Roberts knew him and presumably observed his lack of interest in speculation.[8] More accurate is Gissing's remark of July, 1883, quoted above: 'Philosophy has done all it can for me, and now scarcely interests me any more.' Forecasting the lack of interest that Roberts notes, this admits also what both letters and novels make quite obvious, that there preceded a period of strong interest in

[6] *The Private Life of Henry Maitland* (London, 1912), p. 22.

[7] *The Private Papers of Henry Ryecroft* (London, 1903), pp. 267-268.

[8] Roberts knew Gissing from their student days at Owens College in the early seventies. He was thinking of his friend's opinions at the beginning of his career. (P. C. 1967.)

speculation. *Born in Exile*—which like so many of the other books contains a semi-autobiographical figure in the protagonist Godwin Peak—illustrates in detail the growth of interest in science with its corollary of religious scepticism which was so common among young Victorians and was in all probability Gissing's own experience. Published in 1892, the novel sees the events of a dozen years before from a more mature and more disillusioned viewpoint; it shows Peak's religious scepticism and habit of destructive analysis developing into an all-embracing disbelief (Gissing: 'the only thing known to us of absolute value is artistic perfection'), into an inability at times to grasp the reality of the external world (to Peak distressing, but not far removed surely from 'a great calm, withdrawn . . . and able to regard everything as a picture?'), and finally into a loss of the sense of personality which, with the loss also of moral system, brought about an inability to decide what was the right or even the sensible thing to do. It may be merely speculation to suggest that some of Gissing's own foolish behaviour, the motives for which so puzzled his friends, may have the same explanations as Peak's; I will say merely that this experience of developing scepticism was common at this time. Maurice Barrès, in *Les Déracinés*, the novel which gave a name to this type of character, wrote that the difficulty students of the time faced was to 'passer des certitudes à la négation sans y perdre toute valeur morale. . . . La dose trop forte [of speculation] pourrait jeter chacun d'eux dans une affirmation désespérée de soi-même: ils se composeraient une sorte de nihilisme cruel.'[9]

But if this was the final result of the process, its first effects were less negative. The parallel is clear; of the character Godwin Peak in youth, Gissing writes, 'At the present stage of his development, every circumstance affecting him started his mind upon the quest of reasons, symbolisms, principles; the "natural supernatural" had hold upon him.'[10] Of himself in 1883 he says, 'My position with regard to the universe is that of Carlyle in the wonderful chapter of "Sartor" called "Natural Supernaturalism".'[11]

This is in a letter actually subsequent to his disclaimer of interest in speculation; the inconsistency is typical. Throughout his life he seems to have fluctuated between the pessimistic depression of such books as *The Nether World* and *New Grub Street* and a state which while not quite optimistic yet would seem to retain some belief in the

[9] *Le Roman de l'Energie Nationale: Les Déracinés* (Paris, 1898), p. 14.
[10] *Born in Exile* (London, 1892), Part I, chap. iii.
[11] Letter to his sister Margaret, 15 September, 1883, in *Letters*, p. 132.

possibilities of life. *Ryecroft* effectively expresses the way in which the resigned or negative side of the writer's personality, while dominant, is not exclusive. His fluctuation between the methods of Dickens and those of the realists is similar, but I hesitate to force a comparison.

Comte's positivism was the system that first took possession of Gissing's mind after it had been stripped of beliefs by scientific scepticism, and at first this must have seemed to him to answer the questions and satisfy the aspirations implied in 'natural supernaturalism'. Letters from the beginning of 1879 onwards and the polemical first novel *Workers in the Dawn* (1880) express these ideas with youthful enthusiasm; the novel contains also the seeds of his rapid disillusion with Comtism. Of special interest is the intellectual development of Helen Norman, one of two semi-autobiographical characters in this novel. Like Godwin Peak, she passes through the stages of loss of faith and belief in science; then she goes on to read Schopenhauer: 'After all it appears to me that his pessimism is the least valuable part of Schopenhauer's teaching. The really excellent part of him is his wonderfully strong sympathy with the sufferings of mankind.'

With youthful optimism she, and presumably Gissing, take from Schopenhauer only that part of his philosophy which has hopeful tendencies, and both then pass to Comte. In Gissing, the loss of this latter belief resulted in the statement that philosophy had done all it could for him, and interested him no more; but if Helen Norman is to be taken as a parallel, he had studied Schopenhauer *before* the onset of this lack of interest; indeed it may be that the quietism recommended by Schopenhauer contributed to it. The adoption of Schopenhauer's pessimistic ideas was to all intents and purposes the final development of Gissing's mind. After this he required no further philosophical teaching, and to Roberts appeared to have no interest in speculation. The letters, too, are noncommittal; but the novels plainly show the detailed influence of the philosopher. Waymark, protagonist of the second novel, *The Unclassed* (1884), is an expounder of Schopenhauer in set terms:

> Your doctrine is simply pessimism, with an element of dogmatic faith added. With Schopenhauer, the will to live is the root of sin; mortify this, deny the first instincts of your being, and you approach righteousness. . . . I have never been a deep student of philosophy, but the doctrine of philosophical necessity, the idea of fate, is with me an instinct.[12]

[12] *The Unclassed* (London, 1884), chap. xxvii, 'The Will to Live.'

The ideas of Schopenhauer manifest themselves more or less clearly in all the succeeding novels; partly, as I have suggested, in the form; very noticeably, in the view of life presented. There are many aspects, but of course the most significant things in Schopenhauer are the doctrine of the Immanent Will, manifesting itself in the individual as the Will-to-live; the doctrine of Necessity, and psychological determinism (always an important aspect of realist art); the belief that the world is a place of penance, of constant struggle against always intractable circumstances; and the moral preference for resignation and quietism. *The Nether World* is the most powerful presentation of the misery of adverse conditions, of economic distress, of moral and physical collapse under pressure, of aspirations blighted by circumstance. (This last is entirely typical of Gissing's pessimism—plans in his novels never come to fruition.) There is material for tragedy in some of these stories, and *The Nether World* has almost tragic weight, but tragedy is never in fact achieved. Tragedy is heroic and personal; in tragedy adverse Fate is definable, an opponent, something to be defied. Not man's courage but his futility emerges from realistic pessimism; Fate is not an entity but impersonal and all-pervading circumstance, depriving men of all choice by its existence, providing the motives by which they act, so that they have no power but only the wish to resist, which is futile. The whole is turned towards resignation, not defiance.

New Grub Street provides the clearest example in Gissing of this. The story is of the struggle for a living among minor literary men, an aspect of Schopenhauer's view of life as a conflict in which the weaker (here the scrupulous) inevitably lose; not Schopenhauer's view solely, of course, but the same idea that bedevilled Gissing's century in all lines of thought. Two of the scrupulous—Reardon and Biffen—are opposed to one Milvain.

The chances are that you have neither understanding nor sympathy for men such as Edwin Reardon and Harold Biffen. They merely provoke you. They seem to you inert, flabby, weakly envious, foolishly obstinate, impiously mutinous, and many other things. You are made angrily contemptuous by their failure to get on; why don't they better themselves, push and bustle, welcome kicks so long as halfpence follow, make a place in the world's eye—in short, take a leaf from the book of Mr. Jasper Milvain?

But try to imagine a personality utterly unfitted for the rough and tumble of the world's labour market. . . . These two were richly endowed with the kindly and the imaginative virtues; if fate threw them amid incongruous circumstances, is their endowment of less value? You scorn their passivity; but it was their nature and merit to be passive.[13]

Passivity, says Schopenhauer, is the denial of the Will-to-live, whereas striving is its assertion, and the root of egoism; justice, charity, and Knowledge are signs of the subjugation of the Will and the renunciation of living. It follows, then, that in Biffen and Reardon 'the kindly and the imaginative virtues' should be accompanied by passivity towards the demands of living; and that the energy of Jasper Milvain should accompany egoism and artistic shallowness (lack of the pure perception that is Knowledge).

Gissing was presenting in this book some of his own experiences in the literary world, and so it would be difficult to distinguish this philosophical attitude from 'sour grapes' on his part were it not for further internal evidence. The purpose of life as penance, says Schopenhauer, is to teach the denial of the Will-to-live. Charity is the beginning of that denial, when the ego is expanded to include others; when a man thus suffers the misfortunes of others as well as his own, he must be more than ever convinced that life is not worth having. Life is 'an ephemeral, dream-like, and delusive existence'[14] in which virtue does not lead to happiness, nor does indulgence of the Will. Therefore renunciation, surrender of volition, denial of the Will, is the best way of life; that is the message of life. The Christian prays against sudden death so that he may have time for retrospection, time to receive that message and to renounce life, to die joyfully. In other religions the moment of death is equally important, for the state of a man's mind at the time of his death determines his next existence, and whether he achieves salvation. This is the moment of freedom of the metaphysical Will, in Schopenhauer's terms, the sole moment of choice permitted to a man. 'Quiet and easy is, as a rule, the death of every good man: but to die willingly, to die joyfully is the prerogative of the resigned, of him who surrenders and denies the will to live.'[15]

The deaths of Biffen and Reardon illustrate these beliefs. Despite their large share of resignation, both are of course susceptible to the desire of happiness, which is the effect of the Will-to-live. Reardon says, 'The one happy result of my experiences is that they have cured me of ambition. . . . My strongest desire now is for peaceful ob-

[13] *New Grub Street* (London, 1891); II, chap. xxi (Leipzig: Tauchnitz, 1891).

[14] *The World as Will and Idea*, III, 466.

[15] *Ibid.*, p. 308.

scurity.'[16] Yet he desires reconciliation with his wife, in obedience to the sexual instinct, the most important of the manifestations of the Will. In encouraging him to this, Biffen argues that happiness is worth the seeking. 'What right have we to make ourselves and others miserable for the sake of an obstinate idealism? It is our duty to make the best of circumstances.'[17] That is, they should ally themselves with the Milvains of the world; an opinion which Biffen does not really hold, of course. On his sickbed, Reardon tells himself 'he had the will to live, the prevailing will, the passionate all-conquering desire of happiness',[18] a reflection encouraged by his having achieved the reconciliation. However, he dies trying to quote 'We are such stuff as dreams are made on, and our little life is rounded with a sleep', which perfectly expresses Schopenhauer's view of the matter.

Shortly afterward Biffen commits suicide. Milvain says, 'I scarcely thought of Biffen as likely to kill himself',[19] and this is justifiable. Biffen, as he was first presented, absorbed in artistic work without thought of recompense, quite resigned to poverty and deprivation and contented with his books, appeared to be so balanced a character that one could not imagine him as a suicide; and if Gissing had presented the suicide as one caused by temporary insanity, it would have been incredible within the framework of the novel. However, he presents it as a natural consequence of Biffen's experience. This becomes clear if we think of his experience in Schopenhauer's terms.

Biffen falls in love with Reardon's widow; the sexual instinct is wakened in him, too, after long years of renunciation. As it is the most significant manifestation of the Will-to-live, so it brings the greatest suffering, and destroys incidentally his acquired resignation to the conditions of his life. 'A fatal day. There was an end of all his peace, all his capacity for labour, his patient endurance of penury. . . after that hour of intimate speech with Amy, he never again knew rest of mind or heart.'[20]

Great suffering, as Schopenhauer often points out, is followed by great renunciation. Biffen loses eventually the desire for life. Gissing describes the process in terms that might have been taken directly from Schopenhauer.

One must go far in suffering before the innate will-to-live is thus truly overcome; weariness of bodily anguish may induce this perversion of the instincts; less often, that despair of suppressed emotion which had fallen

[16] *New Grub Street*, II, chap. xii. [17] *Ibid.* [18] *Ibid.*, II, chap. xiii.
[19] *Ibid.*, II, chap. xvii. [20] *Ibid.*, II, chap. xvi.

upon Harold. Through the night he kept his thoughts fixed on death in its aspect of repose, of eternal oblivion. . . . Night, which had been the worst season of his pain, had now grown friendly; it came as an anticipation of the sleep that is everlasting.

A few more days, and he was possessed by a calm of spirit such as he had never known. His resolve was taken, not in a moment of supreme conflict, but as the result of a subtle process by which his imagination had become in love with death. Turning from contemplation of life's one rapture, he looked with the same intensity of desire to a state that had neither fear nor hope.[21]

His death is intended to repeat and drive home the lessons embodied in the death of Reardon; striving to make clear his message, Gissing becomes eventually over-obvious, for he makes Biffen remember at the point of death the same lines of Shakespeare as had Reardon.

III

It is obvious, then, that the ideas of Schopenhauer pervaded Gissing's work, gave it its pessimistic tendency, and possibly also had an influence on its form and method. This is by no means a fact peculiar to Gissing among realists of his time. W. T. Young remarked, when discussing Gissing's relationship to the French realists, that all were linked together by the thought of Schopenhauer.[22] Edmund Gosse, in 1893, made a similar comment in connection with foreign realism, adding with unjustified complacency, 'The Anglo-Saxon race is now the only one that has not been touched by that pessimism of which the writings of Schopenhauer are the most prominent and popular exponent'.[23] Emile Faguet described the attitude to life of the average Realist in this sweeping fashion: 'Le réaliste est un pessimiste radical et secrètement satisfait, qui se réjouit malignement de trouver l'homme mauvais.'[24]

I do not intend to suggest that the thought of Schopenhauer was the origin of the realist movement of the nineteenth century. Paul Bourget said on the pessimism of Flaubert and Stendhal, 'Ce n'est

[21] *Ibid.*

[22] *Cambridge History of English Literature*, XIII, chap. xiv.

[23] 'The Limits of Realism in Fiction,' *Questions at Issue* (London, 1893), p. 149.

[24] 'Le Réalisme des Romantiques,' *Revue des Deux Mondes* (April, 1912), p. 703.

pas non plus une simple imitation, et quand on a signalé l'influence de Schopenhauer, on n'a rien dit. Nous n'acceptons que les doctrines dont nous portons déjà le principe en nous.'[25]

Not from the reading of Schopenhauer alone, but from the general atmosphere and thought of the age, men were arriving at a sceptical and depressed state of mind, a state which rejected morality and the right of the author to judge, in favour of determinism, which accepted the limitations of possible knowledge despite consequent deficiencies in spiritual satisfaction. Gissing, being a writer in whose works personal experience is very obviously present even when he is striving for impersonality, forms a fruitful field for the study of this as of other tendencies of the novel of his time. The state of mind of the nineteenth-century realist seems to have arisen from the sort of experiences described in *Born in Exile*. To this state Schopenhauer came not as a revelation of new ideas but as an exponent of ideas already vaguely held; he would have the effect of explaining the realist's mind to itself. In the novel, his influence probably explains the peculiarly subdued note found in the pessimism of many even of the most vigorous of realistic novels; and he may even have helped to develop the artistic method of withdrawal and objectivity.

[25] *Essais de Psychologie Contemporaine* (Paris, 1899), p. xvii.

PART THREE

Some Views on the Major Works

11

*George Gissing: Poet of Fatigue**

IRVING HOWE

ALONE among Gissing's books *New Grub Street* survives as a classic, a work of abiding value and power. Its historical interest is large, but the claim it makes upon our attention is primarily that of a work of art. Here, one feels, Gissing's deepest emotions are objectively rendered and transformed; here, those impulses to self-pity which mar a good many of his books are subdued to the discipline of ironic observation.

New Grub Street satisfies few of the standards which modern criticism brings to the study of fiction. It is cast within the heavy frame of the three-volume Victorian novel—all too often, with Gissing, the cause of padding, but now used to present a copious portrait of English literary life. The writing itself lacks that aggressive and flaunting brilliance we often associate with modern fiction. The techniques of modern novelists—foreshortening of plot to allow for dramatic concentration, placing biased and implicated observers close to the centre of action in order to make for complexity of perspective, jumbling narrative sequence to involve the reader in a struggle for the meaning of events—these do not figure in Gissing's books. They move along at an even, almost sluggish pace; he relies heavily upon long patches of dialogue; and the events are usually registered through an omniscient observer standing, or pretending to stand, at a considerable remove.

Gissing's treatment of character is also conventional. While there is a strong sense of reality behind his every page, he does not provide the burrowing psychological analysis we have come to expect from modern fiction. He allows the reader to infer the inner life of his characters from what can be seen and heard of them, or he provides brief summaries of his own. His characters are usually treated as if

* Reprinted by permission of the Riverside Press, the Houghton Mifflin Company from Irving Howe, *George Gissing: Poet of Fatigue*, Section III, 1962 (pp. xv-xxi).

they were fixed and synthetic entities, even if open to changes of impulse and mood; the modern tendency to dissolve character into a stream of psychological notation is not yet at work in his novels. *New Grub Street* remains in structure a Victorian novel,[1] but the subject and informing vision are post-Victorian: the setting of his drama is the modern city, that jungle of loneliness and strife. The book is not at all difficult, it is transparent, and to subject it to a 'close reading' in the current academic fashion would be tiresome. What *New Grub Street* asks from the reader is not some feat of analysis, but a considered fullness of response, a readiness to assent to, even if not agree with, its vision of defeat.

The problem of human integrity, how it may thrive or be thwarted in a range of circumstances, recurs at every crucial moment in *New Grub Street*. Like many writers to come after him, Gissing focusses upon the literary life, particularly the efforts of serious artists like Edwin Reardon and Harold Biffen to do their work decently and earn their bread honestly in an atmosphere of cant, commercialism, and corruption. It is a subject with an abiding interest for us, even if some of the details have become dated; but as we read the book it becomes clear that we are being invited to regard the struggles of men like Biffen and Reardon as instances of a problem which assaults sensitive human being throughout the modern world. One reason the book so fully conveys the impression of 'solidity' is that Gissing knew the literary and journalistic worlds of his day with a mordant precision. He knew them not merely in the factual sense which enables him to define the exact shade of malice in Clement Fadge's book reviewing, or the peculiar talent (for it *is* a talent of sorts) that Jasper Milvain shows, or the combination of literary enthusiast and grinding hack to which Alfred Yule is reduced, or the preposterous success won by Whelpdale with his plan for a magazine in which no article will be longer than two inches.[2] More important than this factual

[1] Gissing was aware of the changes being wrought by the major writers of his day. In 1885 he remarked: 'Thackeray and Dickens wrote at enormous length, and with profusion of detail. . . . Far more artistic, I think, is the later method of merely suggesting; of dealing with episodes, instead of writing biographies. . . . In fact, it approximates to the dramatic mode of presentment.' In his own work, however, Gissing seldom approached this 'more artistic' method, and it is open to question whether his work would have improved if he had tried to.

[2] Are Gissing's details really so dated? Would he find many surprises, other than technological ones, if he were to visit Manhattan? For now Jasper Milvain is a television producer transforming the classics into 'spectacles,' and as for Whelpdale, there can be little doubt which magazines he works for.

accuracy is the sense we gain from the novel that the experience it presents has been earned, absorbed, stamped with the authority of pain.

Gissing is a master of place, weather, atmosphere. No English novelist except Dickens so fully captures the greyness of a London winter, the greyness of lives spent under its pall, the greyness of the people who wander its streets. When Gissing describes an afternoon in which Marian Yule forces herself to work in the foggy light of the British Museum; when Marian and Jasper Milvain walk home at night through the dreary streets; when Alfred Yule meets the starving eye doctor at a cheap restaurant; when Edwin Reardon makes his way half across London to visit his estranged wife—at such moments we encounter not merely the depressing aura of a late-nineteenth-century city, but also the visible effects of that city as a social institution, an agency of inhumane human relations. An air of tiredness and staleness hangs over the world of *New Grub Street*, as if everyone were working too hard, not eating well, living badly. Among English writers Gissing is the poet of fatigue.[3]

New Grub Street is a large novel, but not a shapeless or a sprawling one. Its sombre impressiveness depends on a balance struck by Gissing between the needs of dramatic representation and those of thematic rigor. Everything is controlled by Gissing's personal vision of life, yet neither characters nor events are allowed to stiffen into mere illustrations of ideas. Gissing was subject to a temptation few nineteenth-century English novelists could resist: that of crowding his pages with an excess of figures and incidents which would simulate the bustle—but, unfortunately, also the chaos—of human existence. Only a genius like Dickens could manage this without crippling losses, and even he suffers frequently from a promiscuous display of material. Gissing, not at all a genius, organizes his novel on more severe principles. In *New Grub Street* we are aware of the presence of a mature mind shaping the contours of the plot but also allowing the characters a measure of autonomy and idiosyncratic existence.

[3] He was aware of a literary kinship with the late-eighteenth-century poet George Crabbe. In a letter to his sister dated 1888 he writes: 'I have been reading Crabbe. . . . His verse stories anticipate in a remarkable way our so-called "realistic" fiction; they deal with very low life. . . . The description of locality is minute, in a way which only modern prose writers have made common; he delights in the dreary and depressing scenery of the Suffolk coast, in squalid streets, in poverty-stricken chambers. . . .'

Throughout *New Grub Street* persons and destinies are so balanced that one stands in tragic or ironic juxtaposition to the other, and all together embody the vision of human waste which is Gissing's dominant perception. Abstractly, these contrasts may seem obvious, but Gissing handles them with an objectivity and restraint that gives the novel its aura of profound moral seriousness.

A simple contrast is that between Whelpdale and Alfred Yule. Neither a fool nor a knave, Whelpdale has a glimmer of intellectual conscience, only he never allows it to interfere with his demands upon life, and his pliability of character enables him to slide into the comforts and vulgarities of modern journalism. Irascible in manner and awkward in person, Yule is the kind of man with a positive genius for making himself disliked, yet he is also a serious if not very gifted critic: he *cares* about literature, even if with the dryness of a pedant. But this is no mere black-and-white counterposition of venality and rectitude. Gissing sees deeply enough into the destructive side of literary life—indeed of the whole social arrangement—to make clear that Yule, for all his learning, is also a hack, a compiler of encyclopedia copy who has turned his daughter into slavey. Character and conviction may seem to pit Whelpdale against Yule, but circumstances erect a troubling parallel between them.

A more deep-going contrast is that between Edwin Reardon and Jasper Milvain, the contrast between a man of slender but genuine talent, who values the idea of excellence even if he cannot quite attain it, and a man who regards himself as a commodity for sale on the market. This counterposition, too, is not a simple moralistic one. Reardon is weak, petulant, without those reserves of combativeness his vocation requires: something within his character moves steadily toward self-destruction. Milvain is facile and mediocre but hardly a villain, for his ambitions are those of the vast majority of ordinary men and his methods for attaining them no worse than the common run. Reardon allows his conscience to work upon him, Milvain works upon his conscience. Reardon exposes himself to the blows and pressures of the world, Milvain proclaims his opportunism as a gesture of apparent candour which enables him to be all the more cynical. Gissing would seem to be suggesting here an important and difficult observation: that once men have made a fundamental choice of vocation, traits of character matter a good deal less than we would like to suppose. One either drifts with the world or struggles against its current, floats as a Milvain or goes under as a Reardon. The problem of integrity is, of course, related to human character, but in Gissing's view, what character mainly does is to determine the fortitude and persistence with which a man keeps to a stance already taken.

Reardon is obviously the figure in *New Grub Street* with whom Gissing is most intimately involved, and therefore the figure who presents for him the greatest risks. At very few points, however, does Gissing slacken his critical judgment of Reardon, and one may even say that to the extent that Gissing brings out the feebleness of Reardon's will, so does he manage to win a growing sympathy for him. This sympathy rests not on any illusion as to Reardon's power to endure or a concealed identification with his weakness; it is the response we make, at an appropriate æsthetic distance, to Gissing's success in rendering him as a figure of need and vulnerability. And one reason Gissing brings this off is that beside Reardon he has placed the likeable and quixotic Harold Biffen. The two characters represent complementary aspects of Gissing's self-awareness, and the assignment of a pure-spirited idealism and humane stoicism to Biffen removes for Gissing the temptation to shower pity on Reardon. Gissing can now fall back upon Biffen for the demonstration of his cultural and moral positives, and as a result he need not rush, as otherwise he might, to Reardon's defence.

Such contrasts and balances of character help create the over-all 'architecture' of the book. Its local vividness of portrayal, chapter by chapter, is due to something else: the remarkable, almost Hardy-esque tolerance, a blend of accurate judgment and humane forbearance, Gissing shows toward his characters. It is the tolerance not of a writer who has compromised his standards or surrendered to a sleazy sort of worldliness, but of a writer with a profound reserve of experience behind him, which enables him to grasp how *difficult* it is for men simply to get by. Only novelists who know something about the enormity of social pain are likely to preserve a decent restraint in moral judgment. And because in this book Gissing commands both the knowledge and restraint, his treatment of character is admirably free and plastic.

Jasper Milvain, for example, is finally odious, yet he displays touches of consideration for those about him and we are ready to accept his claim that with a somewhat higher income he would be a reasonably decent man. (That is just the point: what he is prepared to do for the higher income.) Alfred Yule is an ill-tempered bully, yet there are moments—as during a struggle with his own sense of truth in responding to Fadge's attack—when he reveals those discomforts of conscience we recognize as the mark, or brand, of the human.

Perhaps the most admirable examples of Gissing's capacity for plastic characterization are the two young women, Marian Yule and Amy Reardon. Endlessly touching in her eagerness for love ('Are you sorry I wear my hair short?' she asks Milvain, and this innocent question seems to plunge to the very heart of injustice), Marian is a figure repeatedly caught in the delicate motions of her feelings. Amy Reardon we are invited to dislike, and for very good reasons; yet she too is presented not as a female monster but as a woman of mixed qualities and motives. With somewhat better circumstances she would make Reardon a satisfactory wife; they are separated not primarily because of her wickedness or his weakness, but because they live by radically different assumptions of value. Good will cannot bridge these assumptions; money, it is painful to admit, might. Amy is to be judged, she is often detestable, yet she too is human—it takes considerable vanity or self-assurance not to see in oneself at least a trace of Amyism. When Reardon comes to Brighton to visit their dying child, her remorse, for the moment, is genuine. 'Hers was the kind of penitence', writes Gissing in one of his caustic sentences, 'which is forced by sheer circumstances on a nature which resents any form of humiliation; she could not abandon herself to unreserved grief for what she had done or omitted, and the sense of this defect made a great part of her affliction.' Yes; for the moment her remorse is genuine, and it is precisely the kind that will soon enough lead her to the arms of Jasper Milvain.

One last word about Gissing's capacities as a novelist. Somewhat like Hardy, he commands in *New Grub Street* a notable gift for symbolic condensation through fragments of incident, bits and pieces of action, that seem to contain the meaning of the book in a few words or gestures. One thinks of the moment when Reardon has just been left by Amy: 'he sat reading a torn portion of a newspaper, and became quite interested in the report of a commercial meeting in the City, a thing he would never have glanced at under ordinary circumstances.' This is a sign of the novelist's true power: to notice so accurately the mechanical conduct of a man left numb by sorrow. Or there is the moment following Marian's protest of her father's abuse, when Yule replies with genuine dignity, except that, as Gissing finely remarks, 'between the beginning and the end of his speech he softened into a sort of self-satisfied pathos'. The last phrase tells us a very great deal about men like Yule. Or there is the moment, soon after Reardon's death, when Amy and Milvain meet each other (at the end of Chapter 26) and without saying anything explicit, merely by the hint of a smile, quite 'understand' each other.

Such details are put to the service of the vision that works its way through the whole of the novel, concluding in the bitter ironies of the scene in which Amy and Milvain, no longer troubled by the memory of Reardon, bask and coo in their genteel success. It is a vision of disenchantment with the values of modern life and, more deeply, it asserts the power of that 'injustice which triumphs so flagrantly in the destinies of men'. This, to be sure, is far from all of the human story, just as Gissing is far from the only kind of novelist we should accept. But from the limits of what he saw, Gissing drew that power of rejection which makes *New Grub Street* a work approaching greatness. There was much in our existence he did not see; about suffering he was seldom wrong.

12

'Grub Street'*

V. S. Pritchett

'Gissing: the English Gorki with a butterfly collar,' says Mr. G. W. Stonier in his introduction to *New Grub Street*. Moscow, transmuted, becomes Camberwell and is lamed. It is as well to remember the Russian quality of our very suburban novelist for, like Meredith and Disraeli, Gissing brings an alien's or exile's unconventional insight into English society. They are all self-created foreigners: Disraeli, the Jew; Meredith with his German education and his Welsh illusions; Gissing living abroad in dreams of Renaissance man and the Greek classics while he listens to the Museum cough in the Reading Room of Great Russell Street. (A scholar, Gissing must be one of our few novelists who is also a linguist; he spoke French perfectly, read German and Italian easily, beside the classical tongues. He knew some Spanish and attempted Russian.)[1] One sees what moods and material the English novel has lost in being written by Englishmen; that is to say, by those Englishmen who, in Mr. Stonier's good phrase, could 'only dramatize their own self-satisfactions'. And we recall that the great Russian novels of the nineteenth century arose from the failure of a class, whereas the English sprang out of its success.

Gissing's failure and his exile are the cause of his fame. We are driven back, as always with imperfect artists, to the entanglement of the person and his work. As Mr. Walter Allen has pointedly said in *The English Novel* the fiction of Gissing is 'too personal, the powerful expression of a grudge'. No other English novelist until then had a chip the size of Gissing's; self-pitying, spiritless, resentful, humourless, his lucid bleat drags down his characters and his words. There is a disturbing complacency in him as he stands at the sink and tells

* Reprinted by permission of A. D. Peters & Co., from V. S. Pritchett, *The Working Novelist* (London, 1965), pp. 62-67.

[1] At no time did he attempt Russian. (P.C. 1967.)

us that life is wretched and defeating, and many an indignant reader must have felt that Gissing was myopic. Like the young Jasper Milvain in *New Grub Street* he seems to raise his chin and talk to the upper air when talking about himself. And then, like many men whose life is shut in by unbelievable domestic wretchedness, Gissing was self-centred and did not recognize that, if one is going in for this sort of thing, one had better open one's eyes and recognize that life is not merely dreary and miserable; it is savagely cruel and utterly appalling. Gissing wrote less of the horror he knew than of the apathy which it engendered. He writes as if he were a mere effect. To return to Mr. Stonier:

> One need only lose oneself in London or in the similar streets of any large town, to experience the monotony of anguish uppermost in Gissing. He respects the low affront, not hurrying, in imagination, to overpaint it with bright colours; the life behind windows does not grow comic or enormous; distance lends no enchantment, and no music steals up the gutters to transform what is into what is not. He lacks the fairy or imp of entertainment; but as the bias of fiction-writing goes, that is not such a disadvantage. He cannot help seeing plain, being faithful, taking the bad tooth into account.

Gissing is very Russian in his overpowering sense of the stale and unoccupied hours we have to lug around with us and this is his peculiar importation into the English novel.

Today, Mr. Walter Allen's suggestion of the grudge is more interesting. In some ways the grudge of several of our young novelists resembles Gissing's, as if Gissing were their perverse prophet and progenitor. There are hints of it in all his work and it is particularly strong in *New Grub Street*. The grudge is concerned with education and opportunity. It has two aspects. Why pass an Education Act, giving clever Board School boys the chance to become cultivated men when they will only find themselves in stultifying and unseemly surroundings and without the means to live in some accord with their minds; and why educate ordinary boys so that they can become the customers for everything that is vulgar and trivial in popular, commercial culture? When Gissing wrote *New Grub Street*, the new journalism with its obsession with things like 'What the Queen Eats' was showing its first signs. Now, it is easy to show that either the competitive instinct or the reforming spirit of social conscience—both of which Gissing lacked—were required of the clever Board School boy in return for his privilege. Gissing resented that only the rich could join the Past. For the unclever, Gissing had somehow got the idea (as Mr. Walter Allen says) that the aim of education was merely to teach people to read books. He was the scornful scholarship winner. (He appears to make one exception in his dislike of the new journalism; in its higher forms of popularization it educates women. One recognizes here the man who suffered from the tongues of ignorant viragoes.)

The grudge of Gissing is the grudge of the outsider. He shows the psychological characteristics in his attitude to the prostitute and the servant girl he married. The violence in these vicious women is really matched, not by the passivity of his temperament, but by what one suspects to be the isolation and ruthlessness of his own mind. Morley Roberts, in his disguised biography of Gissing, *The Private Life of Henry Maitland*, happily reissued in 1958 with a key, by Richards Press, believed that Gissing simply desired the whole sex and, in his self-imposed loneliness and incapable of love, thought anyone would do. One has the horrible suspicion that he felt punishment justified him and so set him free. But—to get on more certain ground—Gissing was an outsider in rejecting modern society altogether because it did not provide a place for the recalcitrant scholar and the pure artist who was poor. The theme of *New Grub Street* is the tragedy of the intellectual worker. The book is a full conspectus of the literary situation done with Gissing's grey exactitude and clarity. The vulgar comic view of writers as a collection of eccentrics is dropped; he catches their fundamental dignity, anxiety and egotism. It is bad enough to be an artist, with its appalling gift of self-knowledge, without being obliged to kill the love of your wife, slave till you are blind, and end ill, half-starved and counting the pennies, behind the tightly drawn curtains of lower-middle-class respectability. The portrait of the wretched, gifted and only moderately saleable Reardon in this book is masterly, for Gissing is unremitting in observation. Without money, a James or a Shaw would just as certainly go down to the smell of last night's dinner in the seedy backroom. Gissing's simple description of the writer's day as he sits at his desk is exact, touching and terrifying; one feels half-elated, half-sickened at the end of it. For, allowing for one deficiency in Reardon's character, the morbid lack of will, the portrait would serve for any novelist.

Those who have the grudge nowadays have, of course, no interest in Gissing's concept of the artist or in his belief in the culture he belongs to. All the same, the conditions of literary society have not changed much since Gissing's times. Journalism, with its short-term shots of success, its weekly injection, still offers its therapy to the writer who can stand the ulcers and suicidal depressions of creative writing no more. Inflation and high taxation have wiped out the rewards of the successful and have reduced the less successful to the role of commentators frantic for a new slant. Our society will reward highly any writer who agrees to compound on his gifts and abandon them. A creative writer must have time. In Gissing's day he had time but little money and, after the first successful start, the lack of money ate into the time. Still, the little money Gissing had was his and he lived in a low-cost society. In our high-cost society we have money, but a large portion of it goes back to the State and we may not invest in our talent. In consequence, we have no time.

Morley Roberts, who was an intimate of Gissing, thought that he shared with most English novelists the ability to create situation and the inability to develop it owing to the national *mauvaise honte* and dread of feeling. But Gissing excelled, as many have, in irony. Each character is solid in *New Grub Street* and if the dialogue is still and the action is slow, there is nothing wooden in the people. Their temperature is, indeed, low. In their varying ways, they are all afflicted, of course, with Gissing's chronic passivity; but in two instances, in the characters of Reardon's wife Amy, and the young, climbing, versatile journalist, Jasper Milvain, he introduces us to two new and disturbing developments of the passive character. Milvain is not passive in his profession; he climbs boldly, cleverly, even engagingly; it is his conscience that is passive. He practises an ingenious technique of self-deception: i.e. he believes that if he is frank about his motives, if he tells the truth, this will clear him of moral obligations. He has the insincerity of the detached. Amy's passivity is feminine, and realistic. She has no will but she drifts with skill. Gissing is unusual among English male novelists in discerning the mental life of his women. Living in an ideal world himself he understood their ideal world. It did not shock him that Amy should resent her husband's failure; and that her love would not stand up to it. It was natural to wish to marry a great man, but it was also natural that, under his influence, she would develop into a creature alien to him and with an intellect of her own. She marries the conscienceless Milvain with her eyes open and with a delicate lack of scruple. Easy enough to make fun of her as a female climber; Gissing sees the comedy but he is detached enough to see she has a right to drift with her self-esteem. She will become genteel. Poverty is over.

When we wince at Gissing's uncritical acceptance of the lower-middle-class dream of gentility and respectability, and at its emblem, the butterfly collar; when we shudder at the tepid, timid ideal world he obtained from classical scholarship, we ought also to point out that he saw people in two troubled phases; as they are and as they would wish to become. To him the individual dream was or could become a serious extension of their emotional range as characters. Indeed, it is out of the soured homes, where dreams have gone bad, or have become ludicrous or catastrophic, that the vitality of this class has sprung. To most English novelists, invigorated but narrowed by class consciousness, one class has always seemed comical to another; that is where Gissing is so un-English, a foreigner or an exile. He sees nothing comic in class. He writes as if it exists chiefly as a pathos or a frustration, a limitation of the human keyboard.

13

The Spiritual Theme of Born in Exile*

JACOB KORG

IN February 1895, George Gissing wrote to Morley Roberts, his friend and future biographer, that he felt his most important contribution as a novelist to have been the depiction of 'a class of young men distinctive of our time—well educated, fairly bred, but *without money*'. Gissing's practice of using characters like these as heroes in his novels has been interpreted as a symptom of egotism, for he had once been such a young man himself. Actually, however, he had good reason for feeling that the poor young intellectual was a key figure in Victorian society. Educated beyond his station in the newly democratized schools and universities, the young intellectual, though capable of appreciating the culture enjoyed by the leisure classes, was unable to gain access to it himself unless he chose one of two courses: that of finding his way, individually, into a higher social class, or working for a revolution which would make the advantages of leisure available to all. Like Hyacinth Robinson in James's *The Princess Casamassima*, he was compelled, in seeking his own role, to make a crucial decision about society. While most of Gissing's early books were occupied with the various fictional possibilities of this situation, only in his last novel on this theme, *Born in Exile* (1892), did he express the insight that such a judgment of society was not merely a choice of abstract alternatives, but a moral problem involving fundamental questions of right and wrong.

Gissing's first-hand knowledge of the spiritual difficulties of the submerged intellectual began in 1876, when, as an eighteen-year-old student at Owens College in Manchester, he fell in love with a young prostitute, and, to save her from the streets, stole money and personal articles from the common-room used by his fellow-students.

* Rathburn and Steinmann, ed., *From Jane Austen to Joseph Conrad*, Minneapolis, University of Minnesota Press, 1959. Reprinted by permission of the author.

An action more out of character for the youthful Gissing can hardly be imagined. The son of a Wakefield chemist, he had been thoroughly indoctrinated with the common lower-middle-class earnestness, sense of responsibility, and admiration for gentility. Though he managed to throw off some of the more repressive influences of his home, and to think for himself in matters of religion, he never lost a gnawing sense of personal duty that drove him to make heroic efforts as a student and as a novelist. A brilliant and industrious schoolboy, he had been admitted to Owens College as a scholarship student on the basis of a remarkable record of prizes and first places in examinations. It seems likely that his repeated thievery was, in his own mind, at least, not a violation of morality, but a gesture of righteous rebellion against the unjust society that had victimized his sweetheart. There was no doubt of Gissing's guilt. He was caught in the act and severely punished by discharge from the College and imprisonment. Relatives of his classmates intervened to have him sent to America, where he stayed for a year before coming to London, a determined enemy of the social order, to marry the young woman for whom he had sacrificed so much, and to begin his career as a novelist.

Gissing's reaction to the new ideas of his time during his years in London suggests that they echoed opinions which he had already formed and which lay behind his behaviour at Owens College. He responded eagerly to the philosophic materialism he heard expounded at street-corner meetings and in lecture halls, proclaimed himself a radical, and gave a lecture before a workingmen's club in which he attacked religion by balancing the claims of faith against those of reason. He read Comte, adopted his view that metaphysical questions were unanswerable and therefore irrelevant to human affairs, and joined the small English Positivist Society as a friend of its president, Frederic Harrison. Before long, however, he found these views unsatisfactory, for his native pessimism led him to doubt the effectiveness of active social reform. And although he remained a bitter critic of established conditions to the end of his life, his fear of the changes that science and democracy might bring was greater than his hatred of the superstition and injustice he saw about him.

The novels about poor young men trying to find their way, which Gissing wrote between 1880 and 1892, form a series of explorations, each coming closer to the central issue underlying their situation. Arthur Golding, the protagonist of his first novel *Workers in the Dawn* (1880), has no doubt that he wants to serve his fellow man; the question that occupies him is whether he can serve him best directly, through active political reform, or indirectly, through art. Osmond Waywark of *The Unclassed* (1884) cynically argues that the artist must be indifferent to questions of social justice, though he cannot escape taking as his natural subject matter the suffering created by industrial poverty. In *New Grub Street* (1891), the novelist Edwin Reardon is the victim, not the judge, of the social order. Industrial civilization rejects the art he offers it, and since he cannot manufacture a product adapted to the demands of the literary market, it calmly eliminates him. These novels, each showing its hero trying to come to terms with society without betraying the claims of his conscience, led by gradual stages to Gissing's most perceptive and most profound analysis of the problem, *Born in Exile*. Its protagonist, Godwin Peak, understands clearly that there is a fundamental opposition between the conventional moral code formed by Christian tradition and the enlightened scientific views he holds. Since he rejects religious belief, he feels that it is logical to reject the moral system based on it as well, for the sake of following a rational, objective morality consistent with scientific truth.

Born in Exile has always been inconspicuous among Gissing's novels. It was unattractive to his contemporaries, and it remains unattractive, for different reasons, today. Most of the novels Gissing wrote before 1888 were enlivened by exceptional social realism and a wide and varied range of interest. They are rich in sub-plots and minor characters that parallel or contrast with the main plot. Though the action usually moves steadily and slowly, held back by Gissing's concern for maintaining an air of reality, there are occasional highly dramatic scenes. *Born in Exile*, however, has almost no action. Its setting is commonplace, its minor elements perfunctory and undeveloped. The plot unwinds through a series of polite and unemotional conversations interspersed with passages of character-analysis. It is reasonably convincing as an example of realism only because its flat narrative style forfeits any other claims. Its one notable fictional feature is the central character, Godwin Peak, a vivid and original personality whose complicated thought-processes are well realized.

Born in Exile was not an easy novel to publish. It was rejected by Smith and Elder, who had been Gissing's regular publishers for about six years. Gissing then entrusted the manuscript to an agent, but it was refused by a number of publishers before being accepted by the firm of Adam and Charles Black at a price that came to only half of what Gissing had originally asked for it. He was particularly anxious and disturbed between June and December, 1891, when the manuscript was travelling from one publisher to another, not only because he was pressed for money, but also because he had hoped that the success of his most recent novel, *New Grub Street*, would create a market for his work. Gissing thought that the reason for the poor reception of *Born in Exile* was not that it was weak, but that the publishers were discouraged by its controversial subject of an atheist's attempt to become a clergyman. Actually, this plot cloaks an even more disquieting theme. In earlier novels of the period that describe a conflict between individuals and society, such as *The Ordeal of Richard Feverel* and *The Mill on the Floss*, the issue is whether or not moral standards can be safely violated. *Born in Exile*, however, questions the moral standards themselves. Gissing's novel is a venture in the direction taken by Butler, Shaw, and Wilde, with the difference that he treats in a sober and conservative manner the conventions they attack in vigorous satire.

The story begins when Godwin Peak is attending a provincial university like Owens College as a poor and brilliant scholarship student of scientific gifts. Ashamed of his humble family and desperately eager to be a gentleman like his college-mates, Peak suffers intensely from the inferiority of status George Orwell has described as the inevitable lot of a poor boy who goes to school with rich ones. When a Cockney uncle threatens to open a cheap restaurant across from the college with his (and Peak's) name in bold letters on its sign, the boy's pride forces him to give up his academic career without telling his sponsor the real reason. In this way the interruption of Gissing's own college work appears in the novel, heavily disguised. Peak goes to London and grows into a man of complex personality whose moral nihilism is too radical even for his Bohemian friends. 'When a man has learned that truth is indeterminable, how is it more moral', he asks, 'to go about crying that you don't believe a certain dogma than to concede that the dogma may possibly be true?' He declares that he sees no need to follow any principle but that of being 'guided by circumstances as they arise.' When a friend argues that happiness can be gained only by following one's convictions, Peak asks, 'What if you have no convictions?' The two main tenets of his philosophy are expressed by two Latin mottoes he admires. He argues that the double standard of *Foris ut moris*; *intus ut libet* is appropriate to a 'half-civilised age' like the nineteenth century. On the other hand, he likes the suggestion of the inscription on the clock in Exeter Cathedral, *Pereunt et imputantur*, that one is held responsible for making good use of the vanishing hours.

When he becomes intimate with the well-to-do Exeter family of a former school friend, Buckland Warricombe, Peak's boyhood craving for the amenities of middle-class life and the refinement of middle-class women leads him to put his perverse principles into practice. Feeling justified in his actions by his conviction that 'truth is indeterminable', he turns the fact that the Warricombes are confirmed churchgoers into a tool by pretending to undergo a religious conversion and studying for orders. His ultimate ambition is that of marrying Sidwell, one of the daughters of the family, for he has heard that young women like her will accept clergymen as husbands, no matter how poor they may be. He gives up his London life and employment and settles in Exeter as a theological student and friend of the Warricombe family.

Peak's piety arouses the suspicion of Buckland, who cannot believe in the conversion of his atheistic college friend. Buckland's investigations reveal not only that Peak is the author of an anonymous article attacking the Church called 'The New Sophistry', but that he coolly discussed the article with his father on one occasion without acknowledging that he had written it. When his deception is laid bare and he is ejected from the Warricombe household, Peak becomes the victim of his own scheme, for his courtship of Sidwell, originally undertaken as a project for fulfilling his social ambitions, has become sincere. He has grown to love her, and now feels that 'It was Sidwell or death'. A final conversation between the lovers reveals the irony that Peak's orthodox role has made him less attractive to Sidwell, whose ideas have been changing, and that she would have preferred to regard him as the creator of a new order rather than a preserver of the old. Although reconciliation and reunion are implied in the scene where the lovers part, they never meet again, for Peak takes refuge in Germany, and in time the news comes that he has died in his lodgings there. At the end of the novel one of his friends reflects that he has died, as he had lived, in exile.

The disturbing paradox of *Born in Exile* lies in the fact that Peak's hypocritical deception is due, not to lack of moral responsibility, but to uncompromising intellectual honesty. Man's life, seen from a scientific point of view, seems to him to be trivial and futile. This truth presents itself to him most forcibly in a kind of mystic illumination he experiences when, during a walk across the countryside, he sees a number of geologic strata exposed in a quarry, and meditates upon the long ages that produced them. 'Escaping from the influences of personality, his imagination wrought back through eras of geologic time, held him in a vision of the infinitely remote, shrivelled into insignificance all but the one fact of inconceivable duration.' To the nonentity Peak feels himself to be against the background of the universe revealed by science, life allows no moral grandeur, but only the Benthamite goals which Peak describes as 'the achievement of satisfaction and the avoidance of pain'. Having learned from his scientific studies the impossibility of ultimate knowledge, he feels that advocating any philosophy of life, even agnosticism, is to claim knowledge inaccessible to man. The only true honesty, Peak feels, is to act according to one's desires, for that is being true to such knowledge as man can have. Thus, his deception, undertaken to gain as much of life's good as possible, is really a moral imperative. "I have been honest', he insists, 'inasmuch as I have acted in accordance with my actual belief.' Madeleine Cazamian has described Peak's situation by saying, 'Il manque à l'honneur vis-à-vis d'autrui, mais non vis-à-vis de lui-même' (*Le Roman et les Idées en Angleterre*, 1923). It is society and religion that are guilty of dishonesty, for they enforce a moral code based upon mere metaphysical speculation.

In spite of the fact that he has thus deftly succeeded in turning morality inside out, Peak is occasionally attacked by old-fashioned shame and remorse. Only through severe self-discipline can he maintain the strength of his rationalization against the feelings of self-contempt that arise in him. He tells himself that his deception injures no one; that he will be able to do good as a clergyman; and that even if this good is based on a falsehood, it is not worse than other beneficent illusions man is compelled to invent to comfort himself in an unknowable world. Foreseeing that he will eventually have to confess his stratagem to the woman he hopes to marry, he tells himself that he will be able to persuade her to share his views, and that his love will recompense her for the trial she will have to undergo.

'Peak', wrote Gissing to his German friend, Eduard Bertz, 'is myself—one phase of myself.' The novel is indeed a remarkably candid confession. The details of Peak's sophistical reasoning must have been drawn from his own thoughts at the time of the Owens College episode and from speculations that ran through his mind when he visited the wealthy homes of his pupils, a poor tutor deeply envious of the luxury and refinement he saw. But Gissing does not seem to have been aware of the ideological dimension of his experience, or of the fact that others shared it with him, until he encountered it again and again in European novels. In works by the Russians, Turgenev and Dostoevsky; the Frenchman, Paul Bourget; and the Dane, Jens Peter Jacobsen, he found young heroes intoxicated by the moral freedom offered by materialism, as he himself had once been. He wrote to his sister Ellen that Turgenev's character 'Bazaroff' exemplified 'the purely *negative* mind, common enough now-a-days in men of thought'. The resemblances of these fictional characters to each other and to himself were unmistakable, suggesting that the nihilism of Russia, the Positivism of France, and the agnosticism of England were all forms of the same historical impulse. Through these novels Gissing learned that the moral sophistry of his youth was representative of a general crisis of the European spirit.

In March of 1890, about a year before beginning *Born in Exile*, Gissing reread two novels which had long been familiar to him, Turgenev's *Fathers and Sons* and Jacobsen's *Niels Lyhne*. Bazarov, the hero of the Russian novel, possesses much of Peak's gloomy and unfriendly temperament, and shares many of his beliefs. A nihilist who proclaims that he refuses to accept any principles not based on scientific authority, he speaks of love, tradition, and religion with sarcasm. He denies the existence of principles, declaring that feelings are the only reality. When he contracts a fatal infection through an accident that seems to prove his contention that life and death are purposeless, he prepares himself to go into darkness. The hero of *Niels Lyhne*, a dreamy and imaginative man whose religious faith is shattered by a childhood experience, adopts atheism as a sacred cause, believing that men must realize that they, and not some vague divinity, must bear the responsibility for their actions. However, after the deaths of his wife and son he is unable to hold to his belief, and prays desperately, confessing the power of God. Later he regrets this lapse, and comes to the conclusion that his prayer was a sin against his firm belief that man's ignorance of the ultimate facts of the universe compels him to accept life without falsifying it.

The French author Paul Bourget, who was a favourite of Gissing's, wrote two novels about men who try to make morality over. The protagonist of *Le Disciple* is an admirer of a 'French Spencer', a scholar who has put psychology on a positivist basis, showing that human passions are subject to definite laws. In an experiment intended to test the speculations of his teacher, the brilliant young student makes a girl of noble family fall in love with him. When she discovers the motives of his courtship, she commits suicide, and her seducer is shot by her vengeful brother. The elderly scholar whose theories have caused these events wonders whether the responsibility for all this suffering does not really belong to the 'truths' he has discovered. The chief character of another Bourget novel, *Un Crime d'amour*, is a wealthy and dissipated idler who seduces the wife of his best friend without really loving her. When the affair is discovered and his mistress offers to sacrifice her marriage to go away with him, the hero is compelled to admit his lack of feeling for her. The effects of this confession upon a sincere and virtuous woman make him realize that his course of action constitutes 'a crime of love'. In examining the causes of this tragedy, he sees that science, together with misanthropy and debauchery, has destroyed his capacity for feeling and faith.

But perhaps the most striking parallel to *Born in Exile* among contemporary novels, and the one which reveals more of the underlying spiritual conflict than Gissing himself was capable of rendering, is *Crime and Punishment*, a novel to which Gissing was deeply attached. Its hero Raskolnikov commits his dreadful crime to prove that he is capable of independent action. Through it he tries to prove to himself that he possesses the contempt for human beings that enabled Napoleon and other great tyrants to achieve power. In his own mind, as he explains it to Sonia, his crime shows 'whether I was a louse like everybody else or a man'. Raskolnikov's crime, like the *acte gratuit* of the surrealists, is intended to be an assertion of pure free will, a declaration that man has the power to step off the path of conduct laid out for him by instinct and self-interest. It is the pointlessness of the crime, however, that leads the detective, Porfiry, to the guilty man. He sees that it is 'a modern case, an incident of today when the heart of man is troubled . . . when comfort is preached as the aim of life'. The criminal, he points out, 'murdered two people for a theory', and Raskolnikov was the only one among the suspects who could have had such a motive. Porfiry's analysis of Raskolnikov's crime applies also to Peak's deception, whose ostensible motivation was far less important than the 'theory' behind it. To Peak himself his action was a denial that the cosmic order had any moral control over him, a reworking of his destiny with the tool of free will.

Thus, *Born in Exile* emerges as one of a widely-scattered group of novels devoted to a spiritual problem characteristic of the nineteenth century. Such characters as Peak, Raskolnikov, and Bazarov may be regarded as striking anticipatory personifications of Nietzsche's doctrine that man is free to make his own morality, and that prevailing Christian beliefs, which favour the weak and humble, are 'bedwarfing'. Certainly, the voice of Zarathustra is clearly heard in these novels. The nature of man's heroic destiny, left vague by Nietzsche, was given a definite form in the minds of many people by the philosophy which arose from the general progress of science in the nineteenth century. The special attraction of this philosophy, as it was expressed in such works as Comte's *Cours de philosophie positive* and Ludwig Büchner's *Kraft und Stoff*, was the hope it offered that human phenomena could be organized under reliable and incontrovertible principles. 'If the Positive Philosophy be anything,' said G. H. Lewes in his *Comte's Philosophy of the Sciences* (1871), it is a doctrine capable of embracing all that can regulate Humanity . . .' 'Un même déterminisme,' asserted Zola in *Le Roman expérimental* (1880), 'doit régir la pierre des chemins et le cerveau de l'homme.' A condition of the success of scientific study in such fields as government, morals, and ethics was the destruction of the theological and metaphysical ideas which dominated them, though they had long surrendered their hold on the physical sciences. This attack of science on metaphysical tradition, which Comte termed the central intellectual conflict of the nineteenth century, is the real theme of *Born in Exile*.

Godwin Peak and the group of spiritual exiles he exemplifies may be viewed as descendants of the passionate and gloomy heroes of the romantic era. Characters like Werther, Karl Moor of Schiller's *Die Räuber*, and Byron's Manfred had made a place in literature for the spiritual landslides which sometimes take place in the minds of ambitious and imaginative men. Nature seems to have followed art in this instance, and the soul-crisis became a common episode in the biographies of the great. The later nineteenth-century fiction treated these phenomena more analytically as the reflections of general social crises. The actual psychic experiences on which these works were based must have been substantially the same: a feeling of estrangement, an inability to share accepted attitudes, a disturbing emotional anæsthesia and indifference to external events. In the novels themselves, these feelings are expressed through an overt repudiation of the external world and its standards, usually in the form of some sudden and unaccountable crime. This pattern of feelings appears in the twentieth century among the French existentialists, who declare that man is cut off from the order of nature and must therefore shape his own destiny without guidance from external authority. They agree with the nineteenth-century opinion that this view of man's relation to the cosmos gives him a new and dangerous freedom. His salvation, according to the existentialists, depends on his ability to recognize fully the 'absurdity' of his plight, and to escape, by this awareness, the imprisonment in an alien world to which nature has condemned him. Unfortunately, such attempts to translate this spiritual programme into action as we find in *Born in Exile, Crime and Punishment*, and Albert Camus's *L'Étranger* win their heroes only transient sensations of freedom and power, before ending in what are, from the conventional point of view, disasters.

Can *Born in Exile* be classed with *Crime and Punishment* as a protest against the characteristic materialism of the nineteenth century, or is it, like *L'Étranger*, a partial apology for the new morality, and a tale of martyrdom? As with most of Gissing's novels, it is difficult to determine exactly what is being asserted. It is not entirely clear, for example, whether Peak is to be regarded as a sympathetic figure. Six months after the novel had been completed, when he was engaged in a last-minute revision, Gissing's attitude toward his protagonist was still so undecided that he recorded in his diary a decision to change his name from 'Peak' to 'Peek', as though he were not sure whether his character embodied the lofty nobility of the former or the hideous furtiveness of the latter. The fact that the original spelling was restored before publication shows that Gissing did not want to demolish Peak's stature entirely. From Buckland Warricombe's point of view, Peak is little more than a clever bounder seeking to elbow his way into a good family. But Sidwell, who sees more of Peak's mind, feels that he is an innocent victim of social forces. The still greater knowledge of him open to the reader shows that Peak is profoundly contemptuous of himself and all human beings, and that his devotion to barren principle is an expression of satanic pride, but the insight given into the painful feelings of envy and remorse that beset an intelligent man arouses some sympathy for him.

Reference to Gissing's general opinions fails to provide answers to the questions that arise in the novel. Are we to accept Buckland Warricombe's uncritical, yet familiar view that the proprieties are intrinsically sacred, even if their spiritual foundation is dead? Gissing was a vigorous critic of this sort of 'hypocrisy', yet in such novels as *Denzil Quarrier* (1892) and in *The Private Papers of Henry Ryecroft* (1903) he finds grounds for defending middle-class convention and Puritanism. He seems to have felt that the proprieties he had been so scornful of in his youth had their value, and that their incompatibility with strict social justice was regrettable. Is Peak's mocking masquerade of religious orthodoxy justified? Gissing's own attitude toward religion varied between indifference and hostility; Peak's fate might be fairly interpreted as a retraction, except for the fact that Gissing remained an unbeliever to the end of his life. While musing on the problems of religious belief in the Ryecroft papers, he wrote, '. . . agnosticism, as a fashion, was far too reasonable to endure,' and lamented that religious sentiment might postpone indefinitely 'the rationalist millennium'.

The moralist and the realist were always at odds in Gissing. *Born in Exile*'s coupling of a strong approach to spiritual problems with an inconclusive treatment of them reflects the rivalry between the moralist's tendency to present his material as an illustration of universal order and the realist's aims of plausibility and objectivity. Like most of Gissing's novels, *Born in Exile* ends by heightening our awareness of moral questions without providing answers to them.

14

*A Novelist of the Hour**

GREENOUGH WHITE

PERHAPS one could not better begin a review of Mr. George Gissing's latest novel, *The Whirlpool*, than by describing its physiological effect upon the reader at its close: a faint, infrequent pulse, a sensation of depression in the region of the epigastrium, an acrid taste in the mouth. It is an undeniably able book, depressing because of its very naturalness, its long-drawn, remorseless analysis of selfish and worldly motives and passions. The 'whirlpool' is the social vortex, wherein a man becomes a wolf to a man, a woman a wolverene to a woman. The question suggests itself: Is evolution, with its materialistic theory of morals, bringing forth its generation? Is an education without religion, a view of life that dispenses with all reference to God, bringing in its revenges? Are we face to face with Messrs. Huxley and Spencer's race?

If every generation leaves and must leave a record of itself in verse, equally must it in fiction also, and in Mr. Gissing's work our generation may see itself photographed. The book is startlingly modern, and its reader may realize and repeat his father's sensations when reading a novel of George Eliot's, fresh from the press. Its style, dry, businesslike, quite unimaginative, is modern, and so is its dialogue; no more of the studied compositions, the choice vocabulary, beautifully balanced sentences and rounded paragraphs in which people exchanged their ideas 'sixty years since', but piecemeal talk, tending to the monosyllabic, fragmentary, with unfinished sentences and questions of artful suggestion. Modern too are its environment and problems—the harsh, heart-wearying roar of city life, problems of marriage and heredity, and above all the portentous 'servant question'. Pathos there is none, though there is plenty of 'sordid tragedy', and the humour, infrequent and flitting, never moves to laughter and hardly to a smile; its quality is *saturnine*, and such, in a word, seems to be the author's mood. Its plot inheres in the degeneracy of a woman's character, and unfolds the misery of worldly life, its debasing suspicions, its turbid, ignoble current. The twofold crisis, a musical triumph and a murder, occurs at the end of the second part (correspondent to the third act of a play), and after it the climax seems weak, inept; but the author would reply that it is the ineptitude of life. The heroine's character is one of subtle, all-engrossing selfishness. One of the prominent figures is a type of primitive man caught in the toils of civilization—the craft of women. A female figure in the background is a parody of the failure of the conscientious ideal, the moralism, of George Eliot. The musical world is put in the pillory; the emptiness of aesthetic consolations is exposed; and 'art' is shown to eventuate in vanity and vexation of spirit. The author himself is impersonal, fateful; too dispassionate to be called pessimistic, and if cynical, his cynicism is veiled in extreme literalness; his only mood that can be plainly divined is one of weary indifference to and contempt of the life he depicts. The personal equation so apparent in writers of realistic fiction—in Thackeray, notably; the romantic element that survived in George Eliot; the eccentricity of Mr. Meredith; Mr. Hardy's rebellious spirit, and Mrs. Ward's didacticism—have all been eliminated from the work of Mr. Gissing, in whom accordingly the realistic movement in English fiction would seem to have reached its goal. And the dispassionate conclusion is, that life for this world only is unspeakably hideous in character and consequences. So it is, perhaps, that the book does open, at its close, the old-fashioned way out: wholesome domestic life, in the country, pervaded by the influence of the Church.

Let us illustrate in detail the points thus rapidly summarized.

Mr. Gissing's method in description is objective, the record of a sequence of visual impressions, as in this interior:

> They went out into the hall, where a dim light through coloured glass illumined a statue in terra cotta, some huge engravings, the massive antlers of an elk, and furniture in carved oak.

Emotional and figurative qualities are scrupulously excluded, and the distortion consequent upon viewing objects through a poetic atmosphere, or haze of temperament, is avoided. Rarely do we find as much infusion of sentiment, and that severely restrained, as the following picture of the hero's departure from his bachelor's quarters

—in which, moreover, a lurid light is thrown upon the problem of domestic service:

> On the eve of his marriage day he stood in the dismantled rooms, at once joyful and heavy at heart. His books were hidden in a score of packing-cases, labelled, ready to be sent away. In spite of open windows, the air was still charged with dust; since the packing began every one concerned in it had choked and coughed incessantly; on the bare floor footsteps were impressed in a thick flocky deposit. These rooms could have vied with any in London for supremacy of filthiness. Yet here he had known hours of still contentment; here he had sat with friends congenial, and heard the walls echo their hearty laughter; here he had felt at home —here his youth had died.

Only in passages descriptive of his ideal—the peace and beauty of country life—is our author lifted off his feet; he is guilty of poetry, both of sentiment and syntax, in the following:

> It was in the town, yet nothing townlike. No sooty smother hung above the housetops and smirched the garden leafage; no tramp of crowds, no clatter of hot-wheel traffic, sounded from the streets hard by. But at hours familiar, bidding to task or pleasure or repose, the music of the grey belfries floated overhead; a voice from the old time, an admonition of mortality in strains sweet to the ear of childhood. Harvey had but to listen, and the days of long ago came back to him. Above all, when at evening rang the curfew. Stealing apart to a bowered corner of the garden, he dreamed himself into the vanished years, when curfew-time was bedtime, and a hand with gentle touch led him from his play to that long sweet slumber which is the child's new birth.

It is time to introduce the characters of the story, and this we will do in the author's own words, and thereby illustrate his method of personal description. He certainly succeeds in setting his people clearly before us, with strict economy of language. The principal figures are brought upon the scene at the very outset. The hero

> had a shaven chin, a weathered complexion, thick brown hair; the penumbra of middle age had touched his countenance, softening here and there a line which told of temperament in excess.
>
> Carnaby was a fair example of the well-bred, well-fed Englishman—tall, brawny, limber, not uncomely, with a red neck, a powerful jaw, and a keen eye. Something more of repose, of self-possession, and a slightly more intellectual brow would have made him the best type of conquering, civilizing Briton.
>
> Mr. Redgrave had thin hair, but a robust moustache and a short peaked beard; his complexion was a trifle sallow.

The ladies are not as distinctly seen: Sibyl Carnaby,

an inscrutable woman, who could look and smile at one without conveying the faintest suggestion of her actual thought.

and the heroine, Alma Frothingham, whose features

suggested neither force of intellect nor originality of character; but they had beauty and something more. She stood a fascination, an allurement to the masculine sense.

These, however, are but superficial considerations; our author's strength is in his psychology, his exposure of the silent thoughts of his characters, their half-concealed, half-revealed motives, their manner of expression.

Characteristic of the dialogue is its significant triviality, its scrappy, commonplace, inartistic nature (faithful to modern habit), yet charged with meaning, pregnant with weal or woe to the personages involved. We open at random:

'I oughtn't to have given you this trouble,' said Sibyl, 'but perhaps you would rather see me here'—

'Yes—oh yes—it was much better'—

'Sit down, dear. We won't talk of wretched things, will we? If I could have been of any use to you'—

'I was so afraid you would never'—

'Oh, you know me better than that.'

A favourite bit of feminine slang is the expression 'early Victorian', equivalent to 'anachronistic', used to ridicule, in a ladylike way, any conservative idea or prejudice—such as that a wife should obey her husband. Mr. Gissing does not seem to repine, as Thackeray did, that he cannot reproduce men's talk realistically; some of his men say 'Damn', and treat each other to whisky and water; and doubtless no sensible person will complain of omissions in that line.

As examples of his sardonic humour let us take the following, at the expense of the climate of London:

Next morning the weather was fine; that is to say, one could read without artificial light, and no rain fell;

at 'society's' expense:

Couples and groups paused to talk near him, and whenever he caught a sentence it was the merest chatter, meaningless repetition of commonplaces which, but for habit, must have been an unutterable weariness to the least intelligent of mortals;

and at the expense of his heroine, and her musical coterie:

> Alma had not the habit of telling falsehoods to her husband, but she did it remarkably well—. . . the years had matured her, endowing her with superior self-possession, and a finish of style in dealing with these little difficulties.
>
> Alma was become a very fluent talker, and her voice had the quality which fixes attention. At luncheon, whilst half a dozen persons lent willing ear, she compared Sarasate's playing of Beethoven's Concerto with that of Joachim, and declared that Sarasate's *cadenza* in the first movement, though marvellous for technical skill, was not at all in the spirit of the work. The influential writer applauded, drawing her on to fresh displays of learning, taste, eloquence. She had a great deal to say about somebody's 'technique of the left hand', of somebody else's 'tonal effects', of a certain pianist's 'warmth of touch'. It was truly a musical gathering; each person at table had some exquisite phrase to contribute. The hostess, who played no instrument but doted upon all, was of opinion that an executant should 'aim at mirroring his own nature in his interpretation of a tone-poem'; whereupon another lady threw out remarks on 'subjective interpretation', confessing her preference for a method purely 'objective'. The influential critic began to talk about Liszt, with whom he declared that he had been on intimate terms; he grew fervent over the master's rhapsodies, with their 'clanging rhythm and dithyrambic fury'.

Our author, it is plain, is a keen and critical observer, who has little mercy upon 'the artificial ugliness of affectation'.

The occupations and reverses of his characters are those of the present day: the story opens with the far-reaching failure of a speculative enterprise; people grow haggard over the thought and the necessity of reinvesting at a reduced rate of interest; one invests in a bicycle-factory, and is involved in a suit over a patent; another converts photography, once his pastime, into a means of livelihood; still another is an overworked journalist, who is involved in the above-mentioned failure. Meantime the women are engaged in social duties and aesthetics; Sibyl Carnaby is absorbed for a while in investigations in the Italian Renascence.

In the matter of incident, one remarks an unexpected likeness to a kind of fiction as different from this as could be imagined—to certain didactic and religious tales, whose authors season their morality, and so excite and hold the attention of careless readers, with a plentiful spice of sensational incident. In *The Whirlpool*, following upon the defalcation, the ruined journalist dies of an overdose of morphia; and there are a burglary, an unequivocal suicide. an improper proposal, a runaway, a case of manslaughter—and the heroine dies through indulgence in a dangerous soporific. Nothing is lacking save a conflagration. The suggestion of vulgar sensation that might naturally be conveyed by such a catalogue would, however, be unfair; for these crises are carefully prepared for, the train of events and states of mind leading up to them is duly elaborated, and they seem to spring naturally and inevitably from the narrative, and to be implicated in it.

The nature of the plot is indicated by the fatalistic symbol of the title. The hero writes: 'I feel as if we were all being swept into a ghastly whirlpool which roars over the bottomless pit.' The heroine circles for a while around 'the outer edge of the whirlpool' of civilization, and is dragged downward with ever-increasing velocity. Note of time is carefully preserved; the dates of the action are A.D. 1886, 1890-91. The plot hinges upon the long-standing conflict between art and domestic life: Part First ends with a marriage, after the claims of the heroine's art have been fully discussed and her right to an untrammelled prosecution of them has been freely granted. Thus the tale begins instead of ending with a marriage—an order characteristic of mature fiction. The consequences of this union are the degeneration of her character and the improvement of the hero's. He has been the surly, head-strong son of a severe father, whom he had feared but never loved; and after a turbulent youth has settled down into a self-pleasing manhood, to which the thought of wedlock and children was repulsive and absurd. From this state of cultured egoism he is drawn by feminine attraction, and is metamorphosed by love and marriage into a most considerate husband and devoted father. He is humanized by the obligations of the new relation; Alma's nature, on the contrary, deteriorates through indifference to them or subordination of them to her artistic ambition, and through abuse of his indulgence. In this character the purely aesthetic temperament, devoid of mental or moral stamina, is ruthlessly dissected. Alma is versatile in talent but volatile in intention, swayed by transient impulses and enthusiasms, dependent upon others' approbation or even flattery for the necessary stimulus to exertion. The only passion by which she is actuated is that of hate of her former friend, Sibyl. This latter name is a symbol; its bearer is the problematic character of the book, so designed and left so when all is told. We do not know whether she is innocent, or an incarnation of serpentine wisdom, of dissimulation so profound that it has become her second nature, the law of her life.

We are indeed left to imagine that the consuming hatred of a jealous woman has cleared the heroine's vision so that she is enabled 'to read the mysterious Sibyl with some approach to exactness'. The motive of this insane passion is Alma's conviction that Sibyl is attempting to detach Cyrus Redgrave from her interests. He is a refined sensualist, a finished man of the world, and the evil genius of the plot; one of his instruments is a Mrs. Strangeways (another symbolic name)—

a lady of perhaps thirty-five, with keen, thin face, and an artificial bloom on her hollow cheeks; rather overdressed, yet not to the point of vulgarity; of figure very well proportioned, slim and lissom. Her voice was a trifle hard, but pleasant; her manner cordial in excess.

Perilous environment this for an undisciplined nature! Alma is determined to use Redgrave's services to the utmost for the furtherance of her artistic triumph, and her suspicion that Sibyl is thwarting her in this hurries her into a rash step which proves the occasion of his death, and plunges the Carnaby's in disaster—but her hatred falls foiled by her adversary's imperturbable self-control and superior art.

Mr. Gissing is at his best in describing a psychological crisis, a moment of supreme nervous tension, such as Alma's on the occasion of her public recital. It is an experience sufficiently common to encourage a novice in view of some great ordeal; when friends apprehend stage fright, an extraordinary, luminous collectedness seems to settle upon the victim.

On first stepping forward she could see nothing but a misty expanse of faces; she could not feel the boards she trod upon; yet no sooner had she raised her violin than a glorious sense of power made her forget everything but the music she was to play. She all but laughed with delight. Never had she felt so perfect a mastery of her instrument. She played without effort, and could have played for hours without weariness. Her fellow musicians declared that she was 'wonderful'.

The style borders upon humour in describing the restraint that society imposes upon expression of natural feeling, the counterfeit of a Christian grace that the civilized world inculcates:

'I don't take offence, Mrs. Strangeways,' Alma answered, with a slight laugh to cover her uneasiness. 'It's so old-fashioned.'

Mrs. Strangeways

was an older woman, and had learnt the injudiciousness of impulsive behaviour.

Alma 'thought it better not to be too abrupt with' her musical adviser. And her husband, having to postpone for a few hours what would have been a severe reply to an unreasonable request of hers, 'grew more tolerant' of her feelings.

In conclusion, the degeneracy of the central character is exhibited by a few infallible signs: the self-pity of the wrongdoer—'Alma had begun to compassionate herself—a dangerous situation'—her opening a letter addressed to her husband, and the unfounded and degrading suspicions excited by something she read in it—and finally, the depth of degeneracy in a wife and mother, a regret that she had not, in her salad days, profited by Redgrave's dishonourable proposal.

The 'servant question' forces itself repeatedly into prominence in the course of the narrative; its crucial difficulty, we are told, 'lies in the fact that women seldom can rule, and all but invariably dislike to be ruled by, their own sex.'

All ordinary housekeepers are at the mercy of the filth and insolence of a draggle-tailed, novelette-reading feminine democracy. . . . When all the bricklayers' daughters are giving piano-lessons, and it's next to impossible to get any servant except a ladies' maid, we shall see women of leisure develop a surprising interest in the boiling of potatoes.

The problem of problems is, of course, that of marriage; one aspect of it is embodied in the unhappy Cecil Morphew, whose life was ruined by the postponement, for years and years, of marriage with a girl on whom his heart was set—because, as he bitterly says, they 'hadn't money enough to take a house three times bigger' than they needed. 'If she had married me when she might have done!' he groaned, after she had refused, on moral grounds, to marry him: '*There* was the wrong that led to everything else.' The problem disturbing the marital conscience as never before is thus stated: 'In acting with masculine decision, with the old-fashioned authority of husbands, [one makes] himself doubly responsible for any misery that might come to [his wife] through the conditions of her life.' The experience divulged in the following sentences is calculated to make the judicious pause before abandoning a life of celibacy:

Marriage rarely means happiness, either for man or woman; if it be not too grievous to be borne, one must thank the fates and take courage.

It is common enough for people who have been several years wedded to feel exasperation in each other's presence.

All things considered, the husband who finds it *just* possible to endure the contiguity of his wife . . . must call himself happy.

Mr. Gissing can never hope to be popular with feminine readers. Yet he represents his hero as virtually *saved* by the birth of his son; whereas in his bachelor days he had been worried by the problem of overpopulation, and had raged against the sacrifice of women to the rising generation, he is brought at last to see in parental affection the only thing that makes life worth living, in the training of his child a sufficient object for the remainder of his days, in the smoothing of its path a sufficient recompense for every sacrifice. He dogmatizes concerning the 'enormous obligation' of parents to their children, is absorbed in problems of education and heredity, studies his child with almost painful solicitude, and becomes more pathetically wrapped up in him the more his mother neglects him. It is the gospel according to Evolution, the only significance of 'salvation' in its scheme.

A dreary scepticism pervades this society; the men, as a matter of course, are sceptical; the hero

felt glad that no theological or scientific dogma constrained him to a justification of the laws of life.

Both Sibyl and Alma attended church, from habit,

and both would have shrunk amazed if called upon to make the slightest sacrifice in the name of their presumed creed.

'In her normal state of mind Alma prayed for nothing'; and the heathenism of her 'religion' is betrayed by her prayers for success, on the eve of her musical ordeal, and 'more than once', later, for Sibyl's death.

From this exhibition of worldly intrigue, of sin and sorrow, dealing death, one turns, at the end of the book, with a relief that one is convinced the author shares, to the home of the Mortons in a country town—a haunt of ancient peace. Mrs. Morton is a wife and mother of the old school, a *true* as contrasted with the *new* woman. 'Into her pure and healthy mind had never entered a thought at conflict with motherhood.' She nurses her children and nurtures them in the love of God and their kind, in gentle accomplishments and innocent recreations. She is aware that there are such things as vulgar altercations and final separations between husbands and wives—but such banal episodes seem to her hopelessly inconsistent with good sense and right feeling. In her own experience she had encountered no conjugal difficulty that did not yield to these qualities, or, in the last resort, to the creed by which she lived—for to her 'the will of God' is more than a phrase. It seems natural to her that a married woman should be guided by her husband's wish.

In this character, whether or not he designed to do so, Mr. Gissing has set forth in fair proportions the perfect harmony of nature, humanity, and right reason with true religion. Unwonted consummation of realistic fiction! With a sigh of satisfaction we leave our hero, a much-experienced Ulysses of married life, and his delicate little boy, their trials over, embowered in a haven of rural Anglicanism—the tranquil harbour of the Mortons' garden.

15

Definition as Structure in The Ryecroft Papers*

JACKSON I. COPE

GISSING'S novels have been appreciatively read by hisorians: *The Private Papers of Henry Ryecroft* has been read by almost everyone. Publicly, admirers and denigrators alike have treated *Ryecroft* as a spiritual autobiography.[1] But Gissing wrote to his friend Morley Roberts concerning *Ryecroft* that 'you will find that there is not very much reminiscence', but that' the thing is a curious blend, of course, of truth and fiction'.[2] Further, an early admirer of James and Turgenev, and one whose own later novels (most notably the Jamesian *Eve's Ransom*) exhibit a growing skill in economically focusing and structuring plot materials, Gissing yet said of *Ryecroft*: 'On the whole I suspect it is the best thing I have done, or am likely to do; and the thing most likely to last when all my other futile work has

* Reprinted by permission of the Purdue Research Foundation from *Modern Fiction Studies*, Summer 1957, pp. 127-140.

[1] Paul Elmer More introduced *Ryecroft* as 'a semi-autobiographical work . . . the fruit of an experience unique in its kind, conveyed in language, distinguished above most writing of the age, for its chastened elegance, its easy grace and balance. . . .' ('Introduction' to the Modern Library reprint of *Ryecroft,* pp. x-xi.) Very similar descriptions recently appeared: see J. B. Price, 'George Robert Gissing,' *Contemporary Review*, CLXXXIV (1953), 109; and Mabel Donnelly, *George Gissing: Grave Comedian* (Cambridge, Mass., 1954). Frank Swinnerton thought highly of the later short novels, but rejected *Ryecroft* because 'Ryecroft's temperament is in essentials the temperament of Gissing.' Furthermore, 'this personality is precisely that timid one which represents the less admirable side of Gissing's work. The book is that of a recluse, of one who has fled from a life which makes too many demands upon him. . . .' (*George Gissing: A Critical Study* [New York, 1923], pp. 123-4). Something close to this analysis seems to be behind Q. D. Leavis's dismissal which 'deplores' the book for its 'mellow redolence' ('Gissing and the English Novel,' *Scrutiny*, VII [1938], 73).

[2] Morley Roberts, *The Private Life of Henry Maitland* (1912; London. 1923), p. 257.

followed my futile life.'[3] If, then, there is not much 'truth' in the book by way of 'reminiscence', we may be justified in seriously considering the element which Gissing called 'fiction'.

There is, of course, the exposition of parts of Henry Ryecroft's career as an impecunious man of letters. But Gissing's patchwork treatment of Ryecroft's past is so rudimentarily organized as to suggest that narration in itself was generally subordinated to the convincing creation of a consistent personality for the first-person narrator Ryecroft. And yet this personality reflects Gissing's no more accurately than Gissing's actual career paralleled Ryecroft's. For ultimately both Ryecroft's personality and the selection of incidents from his career are functions of the larger ordering principle of the book's structure. My aim in this reading, then, will be to describe that principle and to demonstrate that *Ryecroft* is not autobiography, novel, or essay, but perhaps the most thoroughly unified construction ever reared in those borderlands of genres where More's *Utopia* and Butler's *Erewhon* house the marriage of philosophy and fiction.

I

The brute force of money; the negation of the individual—these, the evils of our time, found their supreme expression in the city of London. Here was opulence at home and superb; here must poverty lurk and shrink, feeling itself alive only on sufferance; the din of highway and byway was a voice of blustering conquest, bidding the weaker stand aside or be crushed. Here no man was a human being, but each merely a portion of an inconceivably complicated mechanism.[4]

This, in epitome, is the raw stuff of all of Gissing's major work; the cry of the human soul struggling to escape extinction amidst the grinding wheels of the mechanical world of the new industrialized, vulgarized England. Again and again this typical Victorian theme emerges in his novels. Perhaps it stands most clean-cut as a struggle between man and the modern spirit of mechanism in the statement of purpose by Maurice Hilliard, a young draughtsman in one of the later books who comes into a modest windfall: 'Going to be a machine no longer. Can I call myself a man? There's precious little difference between a fellow like me and the damned grinding mechanism that I spend my days in drawing—that roars all day in my ears

[3] *Letters of George Gissing to Members of His Family*, ed. Algernon and Ellen Gissing (London, 1927), p. 391.

[4] *The Crown of Life* (New York, 1899), p. 180.

and deafens me. I'll put an end to that. Here's four hundred pounds. It shall mean four hundred pounds'-worth of life. While this money lasts, I'll feel that I'm a human being.'[5]

In *Ryecroft* Gissing again sets in contrast man and the mechanical world of the new England. It appears in such unexpected guises as his disgust with Trollope's *Autobiography* for its brazen 'revelation of mechanical methods' of authorship (Autumn XXII); and it appears in obvious places such as Ryecroft's lament at the passing of self-satisfaction among English rural workers: 'The husbandman of the future will be, I dare say, a well-paid mechanic, of the engine-driver species' (Autumn XVII). But in *Ryecroft* Gissing is writing what none of the novels had been: a new kind of utopia. Believing that the frontiers of planned progress had been crossed and that the promised land had mocked the pilgrim with a revelation of factories and tenements haloed by a perpetual smog, he saw that the metaphor must change. If society was ever again to prosper, the map of its ideals must not depict New Atlantises and Dreamthorps, but the pattern of the ideal human mind. Since Gissing chose to try for the impact that comes through imaginative assent to fictional narrator and narration rather than to employ the rhetoric of discussion, the ideal needed a central affective symbol: it was 'Nature'.

Having abandoned the orthodox plot structure of the novel, Gissing did not resign himself to the ultimate destruction of the patrician personality, 'the outcast intellectual'[6] in a plebeian world, as the pressure of his rigid, self-imposed realism had forced him to do in his earlier books. He had only to construct a credible portrait of that personality at its best. To view the book in this way is to see Ryecroft as the vehicle through which Gissing constructs a complex ideal into a tangible idea.[7] The idea is the ideal answer to Gissing's problem of how, while 'losing the [patrician] class', England can retain the 'idea it embodies' (Summer XXII). This idea can be simply stated. The English patrician ideally is that man who grasps the lesson of all English culture: 'follow nature first'. The degree of intellectual distance between Ryecroft's ideal of 'natural' behaviour as it gradually emerges and the explicit statement of that ideal in the eighteenth-

[5] *Eve's Ransom* (New York, 1895), p. 34.

[6] See Jacob Korg, 'George Gissing's Outcast Intellectuals,' *American Scholar*, XIX (1950), 194-202.

[7] Gissing wrote to Frederic Harrison of *Ryecroft*: 'The thing is much more an aspiration than a memory. I hope that too much will not be made of the few autobiographical papers in the book' (Austin Harrison, 'George Gissing,' *Nineteenth Century*, LX [1906], 453).

century shibboleth[8] suggests that ideas and the form of their imaginative 'statement' interact so as to create a *new* idea, intellectually tangible, but obdurate to all attempts at 'translation' into other terms. For *Ryecroft* never parades out the shibboleth. Rather it *shows* the English man of gentility following nature's way in every important area of human cultivation. In its ultimate structure, the book is a many-faceted touchstone by which the modern Englishman, realizing that the best that has been thought and said in the world is insufficient to answer modern needs,[9] may nonetheless learn to recognize and to follow the 'natural' way of life which has always characterized the favourite of nature's creations, the island over which the lark sang, and Ryecroft 'dreamed that half the happiness of his exultant song was love of England' (Winter XXIII).

II

In a preface, Gissing pretends to have found three meditational manuscripts left by Ryecroft at his death. Ryecroft is introduced as a victim of Grub Street whose good fortune provided him with an independent subsistence through inheritance when he had turned fifty. Immediately he settled in 'a cottage near Exeter' where he lived in solitary and satisfied meditation. In the manuscripts, Ryecroft 'had set down, as humour bade him, a thought, a reminiscence, a bit of reverie, a description of his state of mind, and so on, dating such passages merely with the month in which it was written' (p. xvii). Not wishing to make it 'a mere incondite miscellany', Gissing alleges to have arranged it 'into four chapters, named after the seasons', because 'it struck me how often the aspects of nature were referred to. . .' (p. xix). Thus, attention is focused on 'nature' immediately, and maintained there throughout the book, whose structure is 'seasonal' chapters moving from Spring through Winter, characterized by the frequency with which 'the aspects of nature [are] referred to'. It is an extraordinary arrangement if one views the book in either of its surface aspects, i.e. as belletristic *pensées* or as autobiographical reminiscence. Further, Gissing's novels generally are set amid

[8] A. O. Lovejoy, '"Nature" as Aesthetic Norm,' *MLN*, XLII (1927), 444-450, makes a succinct analysis of the idea. Joseph Warren Beach, *The Concept of Nature in Nineteenth-Century English Poetry* (New York, 1936) provides the Victorian setting.

[9] Compare, for example, Ryecroft's observations on his beloved Periclean Greeks, quoted below.

the urban scenes of his Grub Street years; his descriptions of Italy and Greece in *By the Ionian Sea* usually serve only as stimuli for literary recollections;[10] and when Gissing had occupied a quiet cottage with his family in the French mountains, he almost at once began nervously planning a few months in London at the British Museum.[11] These facts are potent reminders that Gissing in *Ryecroft* is creating, not editing or reminiscing.

Early in the book, Ryecroft tells of a trip he made into Devonshire on 'irresistible impulse' during his time of struggling authorship in London. 'Though as boy and youth I had been familiar with the country, had seen much of England's beauties, it was as though I had found myself for the first time before a natural landscape. Those years of London had obscured all my earlier life; I was like a man town-born and bred. . . . To me the flowers became symbolical of a great release, of a wonderful awakening. My eyes had all at once been opened; till then I had walked in darkness, yet knew it not' (Spring IX). It is Gissing's explanation of the structure of *Ryecroft*: external nature permeates the book as subject-matter and encompasses it as 'narrative' frame (the only continuously progressive element being the arc of seasonal passage from Spring to the following Winter) because it is 'symbolical' of the 'naturalness' which Ryecroft is recapturing.[12] Indeed, natural description for its own sake scarcely can be said to appear in *Ryecroft*. Rather, the scene serves as a contrast which impels Ryecroft's mind continually toward a consideration of civilization (most clearly, perhaps, in the episode of the crying boy in Spring III). Perhaps Autumn XVIII offers the 'purest' description of natural surroundings, yet even here one finds that the ultimate comment on a time when it was 'enough to be at one with Nature in dreamy rest' is Ryecroft's inner utilization of the scene: 'In every autumn there comes one such flawless day. None that I have known brought me a mind so touched to the fitting mood

[10] Cf. *Letters*, pp. 278-9, 284-302, *et passim*. May Yates, *George Gissing: An Appreciation* (Manchester, 1922), pp. 46-51 and C. F. Stadler, *Die Rolle der Antike bei George Gissing* (Freiburg, 1933), pp. 34-40 develop the point.

[11] Roberts, *Private Life of Henry Maitland*, pp. 252-3.

[12] Missing this symbolical relationship, it is easy to regard Gissing as an undistinguished scene painter in his 'nature' sections. Realizing that much of the nature description fails pictorially, and finding nothing of Romantic primitivism, Yates gave a remarkably unhappy judgment: 'Gissing had no sense of that fundamental unity between man and nature upon which Wordsworth counts and in which Jefferies rejoices. . . . He has, moreover, no share in the master's [Wordsworth?] attitude of wise passivity to natural impulse. . . .' (*op. cit.*, p. 43).

of welcome, and so fulfilled the promise of its peace.' At one point Ryecroft even implies that his 'passionate love of rural scenery' grew from his childhood room, which was 'hung round with prints after English landscape painters' (Summer II). Further, he admits that 'through my youth and early manhood, I found more pleasure in Nature as represented by art than in Nature herself'. If he has now come to appreciate nature more, he does not love art the less, and the section closes on a quiet crescendo of emotion: 'Let me but come upon the poorest little woodcut, the cheapest "process" illustration, representing a thatched cottage, a lane, a field, and I hear that music begin to murmur. It is a passion—Heaven be thanked—that grows with my advancing years. The last thought of my brain as I lie dying will be that of sunshine upon an English meadow.' This implicative association of the writer's love of nature and of his native land[13] is explained racially when Ryecroft later asserts: 'The characteristic motive of English poetry is love of nature, especially of nature as seen in the English rural landscape' (Autumn IV). And at the close of *Ryecroft* the marriage of *amor patriae* and the natural landscape is so complete that they are inseparable in the heart of the speaker. The passage is Gissing's only description of nature which rises with remarkable lyric grace. It is winter. The rapidly ageing Ryecroft looks out on a 'broad, grey sky, a featureless expanse, cold, melancholy' (Winter XXIII), and his fancy wanders away in 'a dream of summer England'. With minute pictorial detail, yet with sweeping rhythms of movement from county to county, he leads his reader across the valley of the Blythe, Wensleydale, through a Gloucestershire village, across the Avon, Ullswater, then

I am walking on the South Downs. In the valleys, the sun lies hot, but here sings a breeze which freshens my forehead and fills the heart with gladness. My foot upon the short, soft turf has an unwearied lightness; I feel capable of walking on and on, even to that farthest horizon where the white cloud casts its floating shadow. Below me, but far off, is the summer sea, still, silent, its ever-changing blue and green dimmed at the long limit with luminous noontide mist. Inland spreads the undulant vastness of the sheep-spotted downs, beyond them the tillage and the woods of Sussex weald, coloured like the blue sky above them, but in deeper tint. Near by, all but hidden among trees in yon lonely hollow,

[13] At the very beginning the patriotic note is struck: 'I am no cosmopolite. Were I to think that I should die away from England, the thought would be dreadful to me. And in England, this is the dwelling of my choice; this is my home." Spring II.

lies an old, old hamlet, its brown roofs decked with golden lichen; I see the low church-tower, and the little graveyard about it. Meanwhile, high in heaven, a lark is singing. It drops to its nest, and I could dream that half the happiness of his exultant song was love of England. . . .

Not only is Ryecroft blessed with an access to natural scenes, but *as an Englishman* he can live and meditate amid scenes exaltingly hymned by nature's emissary bird himself; England is nature in its most vital development.[14] This virtual identification of England and the spirit of external nature presents the reader with a vantage-point from which to examine that internal naturalness of which the former seemed to Ryecroft 'symbolical'.

III

As I briefly suggested earlier, from beginning to end of *Ryecroft* 'nature' and the 'natural' way of life are contrasted with the mechanism and brutality of the new industrialized England by which the author finds himself enveloped. External nature and 'naturalness' in man are not confused in Gissing's mind; he realizes that man is both part of nature and yet apart from it in so far as he has modified his original state. But there are qualities in those aspects of English nature which he chooses to describe that are also present in his ideally 'natural' Englishman. So the one is able to act as symbol to constantly evoke the other.

Ryecroft's youth in London was not worth living because it destroyed 'natural delights', 'natural joy and delightful effort' (Spring XI). The thought of imminent military conscription enrages him because the 'senseless routine of mechanic exercise' when he was 'drilled' at school had made him feel that 'I was no longer a human being; I had become part of a machine' (Spring XIX). Once he recalls coming on a blackberry bush while travelling afoot, and delighting in the sense that 'here Nature had given me a feast' in pleasant contrast to the 'unsatisfactory, unvaried' dinner he usually knew in the whirlpool of London life (Autumn XV). A speech in a newspaper draws Ryecroft's attention to 'science', which he bitterly disparages for that 'complicated machinery' which makes it the re-

[14] Ryecroft's positive generalization on England's natural seasons emphasizes moderateness: 'Vituperation of the English climate is foolish. A better climate does not exist for healthy people . . . in its freedom from extremes, in its common clemency, even in its caprice. . . .' (Summer XIV).

morseless enemy of mankind'. 'I see it', he prophesies, 'destroying all simplicity and gentleness of life' (Winter XVIII).[15]

Such passages might suggest that Gissing is taking to the primitivistic swamp in which so many eighteenth- and early nineteenth-century students of man in society had drowned. But to see that he is no simple chronological primitivist,[16] we have but to turn to Ryecroft's comments on the irrelevance of Greek culture to modern man's problems:

It is idle to talk to us of 'the Greeks'. . . . Our heritage of Greek literature and art is priceless; the example of Greek life possesses for us not the slightest value. . . . If we should see and speak with an average Athenian of the Periclean age, he would cause no little disappointment—there would be so much more of the barbarian in him, and at the same time of the decadent, than we had anticipated. . . . Leave him in that old world which is precious to the imagination of the few, but to the business and bosoms of the modern multitude irrelevant as Memphis or Babylon (Autumn XVI).

Nor is Gissing a cultural primitivist. Ryecroft is a fervent enthusiast for wild flowers. But he will have nothing of the Augustans' papier-mâché 'wildness'; so, though he likes to see his garden flowers 'growing *as much as possible* as if they were wild' [italics mine], yet he admits that 'a garden is a garden, and I would not try to introduce into it the flowers which are my solace in lanes and fields' (Summer XXIV). Here is a determination to retain the uncorrupted, 'primitive' state of things precisely so far as is consonant with internal harmony for the pattern of *natura rerum*. A more complex recognition that one cannot spiritually go home again emerges when Ryecroft spends a week in Somerset, repeating a much earlier trip. He admires the country so thoroughly that he would now like to live there, 'but that I

[15] Other instances of Gissing's explicit contrasting of 'nature' with the modern world occur in Summer II, VI, XXIV; Autumn XVI, XVII; Winter V, VII-XI, XV. Spring XX-XXII offers an interesting structural management of the theme. Here an essay on the abuses of natural wit by criticism and an essay on the half-educated modern reading public are cut between by a superficially disparate and unattached essay on the natural hymns of birds in Spring. But the bird songs of XXI echo the praise in XX of the natural 'song' of the ploughman which, like the avian harmony, is a rudimentary form of sincere art contrasting favourably with a corrupt public which buys literature only for its 'conspicuous consumption' value.

[16] I utilise the distinction established in A. O. Lovejoy, *et al, A Documentary History of Primitivism and Related Ideas in Antiquity* (Baltimore, 1935), pp. 1-22.

feared the moist and misty winter climate'—a fear which leads him to contrast 'the man I was then [fifteen years before] and what I am now' (Summer II). The older Ryecroft has been withered by his struggle within the pattern of modern civilization, and this debilitation contrasts him with the Somerset countryside which he enjoys, 'those little towns, lost amid tilth and pasture, untouched as yet by the fury of modern life'. If Gissing's indirect exhortation to 'follow nature' is not another of those escapes into primitivism which have wrapped intellectual failure as in a winding-sheet, its real substance must be discovered through the reactions of Ryecroft to the situations of his invented role.

But before inquiring into the ideally 'natural' way of the mind, it must be observed that Gissing implies an important limitation on its scope. Almost at the beginning, Ryecroft warns that for him to attempt to reform society 'would be to err from Nature's guidance' (Spring IV). Much later he admits to anti-democratic sentiments, insisting that he owes them to his knowledge of the poor: 'I knew that the kind of life (such a modest life!) which I should have accepted as little short of the ideal, would have been to them—if they could have been made to understand it—a weariness and a contempt' (Autumn XV). Anxious to preserve the tranquil character of Ryecroft, to forestall any lapse into a high-handed Shavian tone which would destroy sympathetic interpretation of an ideal pattern so ineffable that it can be conveyed only by the reader's seeing it vicariously lived, Gissing has him add hastily: 'That my own aim indicated an ideal which is the best for all to pursue, I am far from maintaining. It may be so, or not; I have long known the idleness of advocating reform on a basis of personal predilection.' But the evidence has already built up by this time. We can accept Ryecroft's humble tentativeness at its proper value. His way would *not* be 'best for all to pursue', because it would not be in the many to carry on the pursuit.[17] Discussing war, Ryecroft finds that a 'natural' human aggressiveness has been so long nurtured in the many that there is now a 'natural' aggressiveness among nations (Summer VI). War is inevitable until nations have done what individuals have more or less achieved through the course of long centuries in sublimating aggressions into talk, into philosophy (again we catch the rejection of primitivism—this time with a Hobbesian tone). But the real immediate hope is not for the nations, but for the few. This section had

[17] Cf. similar denigrations of the crowd in Spring XIX, XXII and Summer VI.

opened with a description of the pacific aura of Ryecroft's own household, contrasting it with those of others who have not 'quitted the world'. Thence he moves to nations and the bloodlust of 'the leaders of the multitude'. But in closing he reminds us of what he has achieved, of what his own sort can become: 'For all that, there will yet be found some silent few, who go their way amid the still meadows, who bend to the flowers and watch the sunset; and these alone are worth a thought.' Here is a contrast between the 'state of nature' of the brutal, aggressive plebeian and the cultivated moral and ethical ideal of 'naturalness' which has been habit-formed through centuries of refinement of the English aristocracy. The fact of inhumane social structures must be faced, and the ideal yet preserved by becoming conscious of itself and its relation to society at large.

IV

While Gissing gradually develops an intimate association between England and the best in external nature, he also is building a series of associations which, when taken together, demonstrate that 'naturalness' as a touchstone for behaviour is a characteristic note of the English spirit. First, Ryecroft describes the pitiful discomfort of an English worker attempting to eat a restaurant meal in surroundings far above his wonted milieu, and comments, 'I should think no European country can show such a gap as yawns to the eye between the English gentleman and the English boor' (Summer XVIII). And yet, he sees in his anecdote a further illustration of an English characteristic which transcends class distinctions: 'the natural difficulty of an Englishman in revealing his true self save under the most favourable circumstances'. In closing out this anecdote, Gissing suggests that we are not to take Ryecroft's ideals merely as dispersed meditations, uttered by an eccentric author set to pasture, but as this true English spirit voicing the aspirations of the modern few who represent that 'moral superiority' once embodied in the English aristocracy: 'To show my true self, I must be in the right mood and the right circumstances—which, after all, is nearly as much as saying that I am decidedly English' (Summer XVIII). The 'I' of *Ryecroft* is not Gissing's 'I', or even Henry Ryecroft's; if not quite the universal 'I' of Whitman, it is certainly to be understood as the 'we' of modern England's intellectual and ethical aristocracy.

Illustrations of English proclivities for 'natural' modes of life are drawn from widely separated areas of human interest. In politics,

Ryecroft argues for the fittingness of figure-head monarchy for Englishmen because they are marked by 'Common Sense' in contradistinction to any variety of idealism. This 'Common Sense' is simply the Englishman's instinctive conformity to patterns which have grown from his ancestral natural needs: 'One of the facts particularly clear to them is the suitability to their minds, their tempers, their habits, of a system of polity which has been established by the slow effort of generations within this seagirt realm' (Summer XX). For 'the Englishman deals with things as they are, and first and foremost accepts his own being'. It is not that monarchy is 'natural' in the sense of manifesting Eternal Law, as in earlier theories, but that it is an organic growth from the Englishman's particular human nature. Like monarchy, England has needed aristocracy because 'the Englishman has always seen in the patrician class not merely a social, but a moral superiority . . . this was the Englishman's religion, his inborn *pietas*; in the depths of the dullest soul moved a perception of the ethic meaning attached to lordship' (Summer XXII). Thus, 'the democratic Englishman is, by the laws of his own nature, in parlous case' (Summer XXII). In looking at the English rustic, Gissing weds this 'naturalness' and its external symbol, nature, in the manner of source and effect. Rustics of earlier centuries were contented, dignified personalities, in sharp contrast in this respect to their modern counterparts, because the latter have lost contact with their milieu: 'The fact that flowers and birds are well-nigh forgotten, together with the songs and the elves, shows how advanced is the process of rural degeneration' (Autumn XVII). Turning to art, Ryecroft finds not only that 'the characteristic motive of English poetry is love of nature' (Autumn IV) but (in spite of 'our modern pre-eminence in the creation of ugliness') 'England alone' can boast of 'the simple beauty of the architecture, its perfect adaptation to the natural surroundings . . .' (Winter XIII).

English cooking receives an extensive treatment (Winter VII-XI), which might suggest Gissing's indulgence of personal whimsies in a belletristic meander. If that were so, the treatment of food would certainly contain farcically hyperbolic *obiter dicta*, such as the notorious statement that 'the deterioration of English butter is one of the worst signs of the moral state of our people' (Winter XI). Actually the discussion plays its integral part in the basic structure of the book, the operational definition of the 'natural'.[18] Briefly,

[18] Nonetheless, it is interesting to see here an instance of autobiographical reporting assimilated into a fictional structure. Morley Roberts tells that

Ryecroft finds evidence of an English 'culinary principle': 'Nothing could be simpler, yet nothing more right and reasonable. The aim of English cooking is so to deal with the raw material of man's nourishment as to bring out, for the healthy palate, all its natural juices and savours' (Winter VII). Englishmen have 'as many sauces as we have kinds of meat' because they use gravy, the natural sauce. Boiled and roasted mutton from an English stove are 'divinely different'; 'The point is that these differences are natural; that, in eliciting them, we obey the eternal law of things'. But in recent times English food has degenerated, the worst being found in London, whence 'many an ill has spread over the land' (Winter XI). Again one sees the tumult and artificiality of modern life, symbolized by the city, killing the true English naturalness.[19] So the paradox is only apparent when he says that 'if any generality at all be true, it is a plain fact that English diet and English virtue—in the largest sense of the word—are inseparably bound together' (Winter XI).

Gissing has set up, then, a series of touchstones which will aid the Englishman in utilizing inherent 'natural' virtues, be they in man, roast, or royalty. However, if the new patrician knows what 'naturalness' means in application, he must also learn to recognize the psychological state which makes the application consistently practicable.

V

Almost at the beginning, Ryecroft says that for him to attempt social reform would 'be to err from Nature's guidance. I know, if I know anything, that I am made for the life of tranquillity and meditation' (Spring IV); from our vantage-point we know that he is speaking for and to the new aristocracy. And soon the theme of 'tranquillity' is taken up. Ryecroft feels that, notwithstanding his poverty-ridden past, 'I can accept with sober cheerfulness the necessity of all I lived through. So it was to be; so it was. For this did Nature shape me; with what purpose, I shall never know; but, in the sequence of things eternal, this was my place' (Spring VII). However, this is

'Maitland [Gissing] with his extraordinary mixture of fine taste and something which was almost grossness in regard to food, loved all malt liquors—I think partly because he felt some strange charm in their being historically English drinks' (*Private Life of Henry Maitland*, p. 53).

[19] Summer XVI had detailed the failure of quality in food, drink, and 'comfort' at modern English inns.

philosophic caviar for the general: 'Could I have achieved so much philosophy if, as I ever feared, the closing years of my life had passed in helpless indigence? Should I not have sunk into lowest depths of querulous self-pity, grovelling there with eyes obstinately averted from the light above?' In thus establishing an intimate dependency of the ideal psychological state upon material security, Gissing is forging another evidence of the continuity of spirit between traditional English aristocracy and his new patrician. Generalizing on the character of 'every Englishman', Ryecroft observes that 'at the root of our being is a hatred of parsimony' (Summer XXI). It is this quality which lies at the base of the Englishman's devotion to the old aristocracy, which he 'made his ideal of the worthy life' (Summer XXII), for 'Your Lord was the privileged being endowed by descent with generous instincts, and possessed of means to show them forth' (Summer XXII). 'A poor noble was a contradiction in terms . . . as though he were the victim of some freak of nature.' That is, the old aristocracy especially expressed the innate values of the English character only to the extent that it had the material capacity for developing the implications of those values in every phase of life. The new patrician too—like Ryecroft (and here one finds the explanation of the mechanism of a *deus ex machina* inheritance which allows him to retire)—must be elected to a full expression of 'natural' living by the possession of financial independence. No more can he be 'everyman' than every man could once have been a lord.

In social relations obedience to his natural 'generosity' has manifested itself in preserving that other markedly English characteristic, sociability. Foreigners often find the English compounded of 'hard egoism, of gruffness and sullenness', while the truth is that 'no nation possesses in so high a degree the social and civic virtues' (Summer XVIII). But the Englishman's way is 'natural'; for him sociability is not a cultivation of the artificial formulae of public 'grace and suavity', 'but as regards every prime interest of the community—health and comfort, well-being of body and of soul—there [English] social instinct is supreme' (Summer XVIII). The symbol of this 'social instinct' is tea-time, 'the *homeliest* meal of the day', because it is the meal sacred to one's personal home, one's sanctuary from a world which is too much with us (Winter VI). As English architecture 'in its perfect adaptation to the natural surroundings' creates 'that tranquillity and security which makes a music in the mind of him who gazes' (Winter XIII), so within the English home one finds the cause and the manifestations of the Englishman's 'old ideal of physical and mental ease'. 'The people which has made for itself such homes as these is distinguished, above all things, by its love of order. . . . With order it is natural to find stability, and the combination of these qualities, as seen in domestic life, results in that peculiarly English product, our name for which—though but a pale shadow of the thing itself—has been borrowed by other countries: comfort' (Winter XIII). Ryecroft recalls approvingly that Odysseus built his house about a tree: 'I am a tree-worshipper; it should be as the visible presence of a household god. And how could one more nobly symbolize the sacredness of Home? . . . Note the tree he chose, the olive, sacred to Athena, emblem of peace' (Winter XV). So 'home' and 'comfort' are for Ryecroft centres of 'peace', the sacred founts of that 'tranquillity' so important to the aristocratic mentality, as well as to all that man has cherished in his weary struggle toward social fulfilment: 'There can be no home without the sense of permanence, and without home there is no civilization—as England will discover when the greater part of her population have become flat-inhabiting nomads' (Winter XV). Industry and mechanization have created the nomads, countrymen who, taught to read the newspapers, 'make what haste they can to the land of promise—where newspapers are printed' (Autumn XVII). It is a terrifying contrast to another day when such people 'had their folk-songs . . . romances and fairy lore, which their descendants could no more appreciate than an idyll of Theocritus.' But 'let it be remembered that they also had a *home,* and this is the illuminating word. If your peasant loves the fields that give him bread, he will not think it hard to labour in them; his toil will no longer be that of the beast, but upward-looking and touched with a light from other than the visible heavens' (Autumn XVII).

This rustic loss of rapport with nature is neatly emblematic of a larger loss, itself in turn an emblem of the fatal shift in modern values: 'It is one of the dreary aspects of modern life that natural symbolism has all but perished. We have no consecrated tree. The oak once held a place in English hearts, but who now reveres it?—our trust is in gods of iron. . . . One symbol, indeed, has obscured all others—the minted round of money' (Winter XV). As he reflects upon this, Ryecroft makes clear why the loss of contentment inherent in abandoning the old English sense of 'home', and the replacement of Odysseus' natural symbol by money are integrally related to one another and to the ideal he is limning: 'Of all ages since a coin first became the symbol of power, ours is that in which it yields to the majority of its possessors the poorest return in heart's contentment' (Winter XV). Again we see the clear head of the idealist. Money as an end has become the destroying perversion of the Englishman's natural 'hatred of parsimony'; money as a means is the *sine qua non* of the new aristocrat as of the old. Living without it, like living too much with it, incapacitates a man for aspiring to 'tranquillity' and sinks him 'into the lowest depths of querulous self-pity'. Like the ideal English climate, the ideal English life is marked by its 'freedom from extremes'.

'Tranquillity' and 'calm' are terms which thread the book.[20] At times this passion for the quiet seems a capitulation to mere passivity, when Ryecroft can say: 'The truths of life are not discovered by us. At moments unforeseen, some gracious influence descends upon the soul, touching it to an emotion which, we know not how, the mind transmutes into thought. This can happen only in a calm of the senses, a surrender of the whole being to passionless contemplation. I understand, now, the intellectual mood of the quietist' (Autumn V). But quoting his favourite author, Marcus Aurelius, Ryecroft reads and muses: '"Consider how man's life is but for a very moment of time, and so depart meek and contented: even as if a ripe olive falling should praise the ground that bare her, and give thanks to the tree that begat her." . . . It is the mood of strenuous endeavour, but also the mood of rest. Better than the calm of achieved indifference (if that, indeed, is possible to man); better than the ecstasy which contemns the travail of earth in contemplation of bliss to come. But, by no effort attainable. An influence of the unknown powers; a peace that falleth upon the soul like dew at evening' (Autumn XIII). Impossible, perhaps, for Ryecroft the Grub Street refugee in his country cottage; but the recollection of nature in the 'dew' image should remind us that it is just the proper balance for Ryecroft as symbol of the favoured 'natural' man of this, nature's favourite isle, the Ryecroft who is one of 'a noble strain, intrepid, generous; the clear head, the keen eye; a spirit equal alike to good fortune and to ill. I see the true-born son of England, his vigour and his virtues unimpaired . . . passionate beneath stoic seeming, for the causes he holds sacred' (Winter XXV). Therefore, as one turns the final page, now with the full realization of Ryecroft as the voice of England's best, one again hears the familiar term—now resonant with evocations of hope inaudible in the apparent escapism of the earlier 'life of tranquillity and meditation': Ryecroft lays aside his

[20] Cf. especially Summer IV, Autumn XIV, Winter V.

pen and, as the fictional old author, his life is ended; but as a personified ideal he is only beginning to live, rising like a phoenix from the ashes of the old aristocracy: 'Now, my life is rounded; it began with the natural irreflective happiness of childhood, it will close in the reasoned tranquillity of the mature mind' (Winter XXVI).

16

The Main Source of The Ryecroft Papers*

Jacob Korg

In his preface to *The Private Papers of Henry Ryecroft*, George Gissing describes as the source of his little book of essays, 'three manuscript books which at first glance seemed to be a diary' where his character, Ryecroft, has written from time to time 'a thought, a reminiscence, a bit of reverie, a description of his state of mind, and so on'. Gissing depicts himself finding this journal among his dead friend's possessions, experiencing the sensation of Ryecroft's presence as he reads it, speculating upon the possibility that he may have planned to publish it some day, and then deciding to edit and publish it himself as the volume of essays which the reader has in his hand. Such a manuscript source of the Ryecroft Papers actually exists; it is a holograph notebook of about sixty-five pages now in the Henry W. and Albert A. Berg Collection of The New York Public Library.

The Berg notebook does not correspond very well with the fictional one described in Gissing's preface. It is one volume, not three, and it is not a diary, but a Commonplace Book. Gissing actually did keep a three-volume diary (it is also in the Berg Collection), but it was used to record daily events, and is not related to the Ryecroft Papers, while the Commonplace Book, which was reserved for the purposes mentioned by Gissing, as well as for recording outlines and extracts of reading, contains much of the material in the Ryecroft Papers, and is obviously the original of the manuscript described in the preface. Its entries are not dated by months as those in Ryecroft's diary are supposed to be, and they are not in the form of the well-developed short essays found in the Ryecroft Papers, but are, with a few exceptions, brief observations on memoranda which had to be expanded before they could be used in the published volume.

* Reprinted from Jacob Korg, introduction to *George Gissing's Commonplace Book*, the New York Public Library, 1962, pp. 7-16, by permission of the author.

Several pages have been cut out of the front of the notebook, but the numbering of the remaining pages begins with 1. Though the entries are undated, the incidental dates which appear show that the Commonplace Book was begun about July 1887 and continued past the publication of *Ryecroft* until the year of Gissing's death, 1903. The first fifty pages are occupied by Gissing's notes, few of them, except for extracts or summaries of reading, longer than three or four lines. There follow five unnumbered pages of short entries in the script of Gabrielle Fleury, Gissing's third wife, which are headed 'Some Remarks of G.G.', and which were apparently written after his death. The pages at the back of the notebook contain miscellaneous notes: summaries of reading, a list of cancelled book-titles, a page of quotations from book-reviews, 'Names for Stories' (most of them cancelled), some comments on the behaviour of his first son as a child, a glossary of unusual words with definitions and quotations, and a listing of 'My favourite books'.

The Commonplace Book was obviously Gissing's familiar, equally appropriate for recording snatches of conversation heard in the street, or meditations about the servant problem, and for noting a relationship between an opinion of Aristotle and the Sermon on the Mount. The mind revealed by these random and informal notes ranges widely through history and the literatures of several languages, but it is capable of stumbling over trivial immediate problems of domestic economy and family relations. At the same time, however, it finds the local and particular more congenial than the general. Gissing is excellent when he is touching the end of some significant filament of thought, and feeling gently along its length to sense its implications, but he usually fails when he seeks to muster the ingenuity necessary for framing a conclusive aphorism or witticism. Entries intended to be pithy or epigrammatic, such as the one about the workman building his own scaffold, are nearly always naïve, obvious, and ineffective. The Commonplace Book contains much outline, quotation, and summary, but very little extended analysis. Even when allowances are made for the fact that a notebook of this type is usually used for recording reading, the disproportion between these two elements strengthens the general impression created by its contents. It is the product of a comparatively passive mind, whose excellences are sensitivity, patience and responsiveness rather than energy or a gift for invention. It is a mind which can be seen lying in wait to catch the telling contrast, the significant gesture or the stylistic peculiarity, both in reading and in daily experience. Even the vigorous attacks upon the barbarism of the times which are found in the Commonplace Book are results of irritation rather than sustained critical thought. In short, these are the reflections of a contemplative, lingering sensibility, equally responsive to beauty and incongruity, which is capable of energetic protest when its calm is disturbed by some encounter with stupidity, vulgarity, or injustice.

Readers familiar with Gissing's novels will recognize in the Commonplace Book the unusual combination of tastes and attitudes characteristic of him. The social criticism of his novels often gives the impression that he was by nature a controversialist and reformer, but his real preferences were privacy, meditation, and quiet reading. He was essentially a bibliophile with an active social conscience. As Samuel V. Gapp has pointed out in his study of Gissing's classical side, he is the unique case of an author whose two major interests were slum life and classical antiquity; he was equally drawn to the metrical and linguistic refinements of Greek and Latin poetry, and to the sufferings of the women and children he saw in the London slums. The contradictions sometimes evident in Gissing's opinions are due to the fact that he was committed to irreconcilable extremes of humanism and humanitarianism. His novels are constantly occupied with contemporary social problems, but he approached them, when his views became settled, with profoundly traditional convictions. In some respects, to be sure, he was a man of his century. He had had an early socialist period, he was an agnostic, a pacifist, a feminist, and, in his fiction, a realist; he was contemptuous of supernatural beliefs, and did not accept conventional ideas of sexual morality or woman's place in society. But he distrusted most of the dominant tendencies of his time, including science, democracy, social planning, philanthropy, and popular education.

The Commonplace Book echoes the pessimism of Gissing's social novels, but it also reveals a feeling not often apparent in them: compassion. The sadness which invariably overtook Gissing when he contemplated the human condition appears in the entry where he says that he enjoys watching a puppy at play, but takes no pleasure in babies, because he thinks of the suffering they will grow up to experience. The deep-rooted unwillingness of people to throw away left-over bits of bread reminds him of the hardships of the struggle for survival. He is strongly moved by the plight of the piano prodigy, Josef Hofmann, who protested against the demands made upon him, that he was 'only a little boy'. Innumerable passages of his novels are critical of the poor, and in the Ryecroft Papers, Gissing explicitly sets himself apart from them, but one of the entries of the Commonplace Book, in which he reports that comparing his own hands with those of a working man or woman makes him feel 'deeply wretched', reveals his latent sense of guilt, and his capacity for an inarticulate, agonizing sympathy. The Commonplace Book, like the novels, shows that Gissing is most easily aroused to sympathy by the spectacle of suffering women. He is outraged to learn that women in Russia are forced to sell their hair under the pressure of famine, and reports that he is always infuriated, when he reads *Pendennis*, at the behaviour of Mrs. Pendennis toward Fanny Bolton. The one essay of some length in the Commonplace Book, an argument against the death penalty, was occasioned by the execution of a woman.

The Commonplace Book contains abundant social criticism of the kind found in Gissing's novels. As a confirmed opponent of the monetary standards by which worth is measured in a materialist society, he saw a deep significance in the fact that he had once satisfied his hunger without payment by eating blackberries picked at the roadside (an episode mentioned in *The Private Papers of Henry Ryecroft*), and he was able to share the amusement of a Kafir he read of who learned that a man could starve to death in a civilized country if he lacked the money to buy food. His opposition to what is generally called progress is savagely expressed in his satisfaction at the death of a man who ventured aloft in an early flying machine. Gissing's critical tendencies were acutely responsive to the small ironies of everyday life. Conversational banalities, journalistic solecisms, and the vulgar behaviour of royalty and nobility are often noted in the Commonplace Book. Typical of the disillusioning experiences to which his critical instincts subjected him was the discussion with Eduard Bertz about a passage in George Eliot, which forced Gissing to conclude that Bertz's judgment, intelligent as it may have been, was severely limited by chauvinism and prudery.

Though it contains few references to events in Gissing's life, the Commonplace Book does give some factual information which augments the main biographical sources, Morley Roberts's *Private Life of Henry Maitland*, and Gissing's *Letters to Members of His Family*. One entry mentions an inability to open his mind fully to his relations, suggesting that the volume of letters, most of them addressed to his brothers and sisters, is of only limited value as a revelation of his thoughts. Other entries recall experiences related to his lifelong feeling that he was a social exile: the loneliness of his childhood, dreams of being unable to communicate with his father, his aversion to large dinner parties and casual social intercourse. Gissing attributed his difficulty in communicating with his family to a general reserve about sexual matters, but he also differed with them on religious questions, and the Commonplace Book often reflects his agnostic convictions. The various entries show that he was critical of the intellectual rather than the emotional side of religion. He says he has no objection to religious feeling, and he actually remarks on the beauty of a chapter in Genesis, but he records instances of religious casuistry which he encountered in his reading with something approaching horror.

Though the love of Italy, anti-democratic prejudices, misogyny, and opposition to religion which frequently appear in Gissing's fiction are clearly recognizable in the Commonplace Book, it contains surprisingly few references to his novels, and has few direct relationships with them. He used it to make note of the motto, *Foris ut moris, intus ut libet*, which Godwin Peak, the hero of *Born in Exile*, adopts as a principle, and to write down an amusing advertiser's slogan for Beecham's pills which appears in *In the Year of Jubilee*. The notes for his novels to which his letters and diary refer were made elsewhere, and if they survive, have not yet appeared among the manuscripts in the possession of American libraries. But if the Commonplace Book can claim only the sort of general relationship to Gissing's novels which is natural to texts written by the same author and reflecting the same attitudes, it is very closely related to his best-known book, *The Private Papers of Henry Ryecroft*. It is not surprising that the Commonplace Book and the Ryecroft Papers should have much of their material in common. The Commonplace Book is, after all, the actual counterpart of the fictional Ryecroft Papers; it is what the Ryecroft Papers would be if Gissing had published his own notes instead of those of a *persona* closely resembling himself. Critics have often warned that the Ryecroft Papers are not autobiographical, but the Commonplace Book shows that they are, to a greater extent than it has hitherto been possible to determine, an accurate expression of Gissing's views.

This is not to say that Ryecroft is identical with Gissing. He is a fictional character, clearly distinguishable in several respects from his author, a retired writer of articles and translations living in Devon on a small competence alone, except for a housekeeper. Gissing did not feel that his literary work was worthless, as Ryecroft does, did not share Ryecroft's willingness to let what he had written slip into oblivion, and never achieved the quiet life of placid resignation which sets the tone of the book as a whole. Writing to his friend, Frederic Harrison, of his little volume of essays, Gissing said that he hoped it would not be regarded as autobiographical, for 'The thing is much more an aspiration than a memory'.[1]

The similarities between Gissing's private opinions as they are found in the Commonplace Book and those of his character, Ryecroft, make it clear that Gissing's volume of essays represents the emergence of a tendency. always latent in his novels, to subordinate fictional values to ideological ones. The rivalry between legitimate narrative interests and didactic and autobiographical motivations creates a sense of strain in most of Gissing's novels, though the former usually do succeed in holding their ground. The Ryecroft Papers, it now seems clear, are a reversal of the balance, and a yielding to long-suppressed ambitions. More essay than novel, they contain freely-elaborated discursive and autobiographical materials, while the fictional elements are reduced to a single character and a single setting which provide a structural framework for what would otherwise have been a series of unrelated essays.

The Commonplace Book was not a first draft of the Ryecroft Papers, for it was not intended for publication, but there can be little doubt that Gissing had it before him when he wrote his book of essays in the fall of 1900. Ryecroft himself actually mentions the Commonplace Book, for it is the 'old notebook' to which he refers as the place where he wrote a list of ambitions as a young man. On the other hand, the Commonplace Book records an intention, conceived at least thirteen years earlier, to write the book of essays which eventually became the Ryecroft Papers. In writing his essays, Gissing used many of the quotations and observations he had noted in the Commonplace Book, sometimes making hardly any changes in his original note, sometimes expanding it into an entire essay. In one or two cases the sense of his entry, as it found its way into the Ryecroft Papers, is markedly different from the original one, and these divergencies, showing as they do, shifts of opinion in Gissing's mind, are of particular interest.

Perhaps the best evidence offered by the Commonplace Book to support the view that the Ryecroft Papers are largely confessional is the fact that it shows many of Ryecroft's personal tastes and reactions, which might otherwise be considered mere characterizing

[1] From an unpublished letter dated 11 February 1903, in the collection of the Pforzheimer Library.

details, to be authentic parts of Gissing's personality. This is true of Ryecroft's antipathy to vegetarianism and his account of a vegetarian phase in his youth; the Commonplace Book mentions the vegetable diet to which Gissing once resorted in an attempt to economize, and the animosity he bore toward 'haricots and lentils' ever afterward is recorded by Gabrielle. When Ryecroft sees a pencilled inscription eighty years old in a Latin volume bought at a secondhand bookshop, he experiences a feeling of identity with the former owner. Gissing had had such an experience with the same book—a copy of Tibullus—and had described it to Gabrielle, who noted it as one of her 'remarks': 'The pathos of old signatures & bookplates in 2[d] hand vol. At end of my Tibullus: *Perlegi.*' Ryecroft's report that he suffered from the longing for Italy described by Goethe in his *Italienische Reise* is another experience of Gissing's which is recorded on page 14 of the Commonplace Book. Ryecroft has an odd taste for articles describing exhibitions of landscape paintings, for the names of the canvases arouse his imagination and enable him to picture country scenes; this, according to Gabrielle's notes, is also one of Gissing's traits. The sensitive, yet severely disciplined essay of Autumn XXIII, in which Ryecroft has a sudden insight into the futility of his life, is drawn from Gissing's own feelings, expressed to Gabrielle, and recorded by her, in scattered phrases, in the Commonplace Book. In Spring XX Ryecroft reflects that he has never found anyone so sympathetic with his temperament that he could read aloud to him with confidence that his appreciation would be shared; the same test of understanding is mentioned by Gissing on page 18 of the Commonplace Book as an illustration of his exceptional need for sympathy. Numerous parallels of this kind show that while Gissing may have invented a fictional character in Ryecroft, he did not invent a personality for him, but supplied him with his own.

There has never been much doubt that Ryecroft's opinions are identical with Gissing's, for they harmonize very well with the ideas expressed in the novels, and the Commonplace Book corroborates the general accuracy of this view. Gissing's chronic impatience with the barbarism of an age he regarded as cursed by the twin evils of industrialism and democracy is one of the most frequent themes of his Commonplace Book, as it is of the Ryecroft Papers. The notebook from which Ryecroft copied the list of policemen who were needed to keep order at a race-meeting in Spring XIV is, of course, the Commonplace Book, where the list appears on page 42. The quotation reproduced in Spring XV from an insensitive woman's brutal account of her lion-hunting exploits appears in the Commonplace Book. The definition of art as an expression of 'the zest of life' was something Gissing himself had said, for it is recorded as one of his 'remarks' by Gabrielle. In Spring XXII, Gissing seeks to account for the persistence of barbarism in an advanced and civilized age by the argument that intellectual development does not necessarily affect taste or morality. This discussion is related to certain scenes in his novels *Thyrza* and *In the Year of Jubilee* which suggest that mass education is futile, for it cannot change the essential vulgarity of the proletarian. In a society dedicated to educating its future masters, Gissing was one of the few who denied that education must have ennobling effects. Perhaps the earliest record of this opinion, to which he reverted frequently in criticizing one of the favourite panaceas of contemporary reform, is the note from Ribot beginning, 'The personal influence of education is trivial'.

Gissing was opposed to egalitarianism. Being particularly sensitive to the proprieties of dress, manners and speech, he was convinced that the social deficiencies of the poor were symptoms of their radical defects of spirit and morality. This prejudice of Gissing's is an extreme specialization of the view to which, it has been said, the English novel as a whole is committed, the view that reality is to be found in the sphere of social life. Gissing saw an excellent example of the unalterable inferiority of the lower classes in the anecdote recorded in the Commonplace Book about the young workman who ventured into a good restaurant, only to find himself totally at a loss in an alien environment, and unable to eat his meal. The story was rewritten, and used with a similar interpretation in Summer XVII in the Ryecroft Papers.

Many of the Commonplace Book's brief entries are germs of thought which were later amplified into the meditations of the Ryecroft Papers. A plan for comparing educated and uneducated attitudes toward honey became the essay of Summer XIX which describes how common experiences in general can be enriched by literary associations. In another note Gissing observes that a man calling in a field reminded him of a peasant he had heard singing in Italy; this event and the sensation it aroused are fully described in Autumn XIX. An impatient remark about Trollope's revelation, in his *Autobiography*, of the mechanical way in which he had written his novels, recorded in the Commonplace Book by Gabrielle, is expanded into the discussion of Autumn XXII, where Ryecroft wonders whether much-needed reforms in the methods of publishing will not harm literature. Summer XXVI, which describes the intense pleasure Ryecroft experiences at overhearing piano music in an Exeter street, has as its germ an entry on page 9 of the Commonplace Book. The chief details of Winter VI, a charming celebration of the rite of tea, appear in one entry in detached phrases. And the most striking part of the meditation on death of Autumn XII, the idea that death forms a bond among men because all have to suffer it, is based upon another short Commonplace Book entry.

In Winter XVII Ryecroft asks himself why he spends so much time reading history, and the answer he gives to this question involves a number of reflections which are found scattered through the Commonplace Book, thus showing again that in *Ryecroft* Gissing was writing from his own mind, not from a fictional one. Ryecroft is unable to explain his taste. 'History', he says, 'is a nightmare of horrors,' and he tells himself that he would be better advised to devote his few remaining days to literature. In the Commonplace Book, however, Gissing has an answer to the same question which parallels Ryecroft's aversion. 'My pleasure in reading history', he says, 'arises from the thought that these things are all over, & the people at rest.' Among the things that disturb Ryecroft about history is the awareness that in the course of the world's long story very many people have been deliberately tortured to death. The sensitive and morbid Gissing confesses, in the Commonplace Book, that the thought of all the physical pain human beings have undergone often comes as a torment to him. 'These things', he wrote, 'haunt me in the night.' Ryecroft concludes that his time for acquiring new knowledge is over, and that it is as futile for him to study history as it would be to try to learn a new language. But one of the very last notes in the Commonplace Book shows that Gissing reconsidered the question of language study, for he mentions the case of Conrad as evidence against the view that one cannot learn a new language 'in mature years'.

There are, in fact, a number of interesting differences between the views of Ryecroft and those expressed by Gissing himself in the Commonplace Book, but it is safe to say that they do not for the most part compromise the authenticity of the Ryecroft Papers as a personal confession, but represent shifts of opinion on Gissing's part. The wording of a sign describing an excursion steamer as 'replete with lavatories' appears in the Commonplace Book with an enraged comment calling for the arrest of the man guilty of this solecism, but in the Ryecroft Papers it is presented, more tolerantly, as a subject for laughter. In the Commonplace Book Gissing recorded Hawthorne's comment that work was 'the curse of the world' with approval. By the time it found its way into the Ryecroft Papers, however, it had become the germ of an elaborate reflection on the condition of agricultural labourers, and Gissing no longer agreed with it.

Gissing's attitude toward the common people, always unsettled and indecisive, is the subject of the one really sharp divergence between the opinions of the Ryecroft Papers and those of the Commonplace Book. *Ryecroft* was written in what might be called the third stage of Gissing's inconclusive and lifelong struggle with this problem. He had originally thought of himself as a partisan of the poor, or, at least, of the best among them, as such novels as *Workers in the Dawn* and *Thyrza* show, but after his first trip to the Continent, he grew indifferent to poverty and its problems, and turned to novels of middle-class life, referring to the lower classes only in order to renew his warnings against the danger of the growing power of democracy. Toward the end of his life, however, a softening of his hostility became evident. Perhaps the turning point was the period of illness at Cotrone in the winter of 1897 which is described in *By the Ionian Sea* when, during his confinement to his room in a simple inn, he was forced to observe the servants who waited on him, and noticed that, in spite of their rough and tattered appearance, they were essentially kind and amiable. Gissing's last completed novel, *Will Warburton*, suggests that there are worse fates than identification with the lower middle class, for at the end its hero accepts the status and motivations of a grocer, and the Ryecroft Papers have some passages on the poor which are not only sympathetic, but, more significantly, respectful and affectionate.

If this evolution of attitudes represented Gissing's development fully, it would be possible to conclude that he had finally come to terms with the problem. But the entries on the common people and democracy in the Commonplace Book are uniformly hostile. The two Jubilees held in 1887 and 1897 in honour of the fiftieth and sixtieth anniversaries of Victoria's succession to the throne were public festivals which drew great crowds to the centre of London. In his novel *In the Year of Jubilee*, Gissing uses these crowds as a symbol of the brutality of the masses of people; both Jubilee days are mentioned in the Commonplace Book, and both occasion savage anti-democratic criticism. Yet Summer XX in the Ryecroft Papers is an essay on the Jubilee of 1897 which celebrates 'a legitimate triumph of the average man', and praises the humble virtues and social progress of 'the People'. One is tempted to conclude that this essay, unlike the rest of the Ryecroft Papers, represents Ryecroft's point of view, not Gissing's, and that it is intended to reflect the patient and resigned temperament of Gissing's fictional character, not to express his own very different opinion.

Ryecroft's placid resignation is a mood which Gissing himself did not share, as the Commonplace Book and some of his letters written late in life clearly show. Like Ryecroft, he felt that he could face death without fear; but he could not accept the evils of life without rancour, as Ryecroft can. In his last years Gissing continued to express grievances over the sale of his books, and to grumble about women, society, and the reviewers. In one entry he regrets his inability to undergo humiliation calmly; in another (whose phraseology appears in the Ryecroft Papers) he calls resignation, Ryecroft's source of strength, 'one of the most pathetic things'. Thus, the tone of calm melancholy which is one of the most attractive features of the Ryecroft Papers is not an expression of Gissing's feelings, but an effort of his imagination. Ryecroft's acceptance of the world's neglect was something he could realize in writing, but could not bring himself to feel. It was no doubt the quality of Ryecroft's mind to which, in the midst of the hostilities and resentments he recorded in his Commonplace Book, he most fervently aspired.

Index

Note: Insignificant allusions to subjects, authors or characters have not been recorded. Female characters are to be found under their Christian names, when any; male characters under their surnames.

O

P

Q

R

S

T

For Product Safety Concerns and Information please contact our EU representative GPSR@taylorandfrancis.com
Taylor & Francis Verlag GmbH, Kaufingerstraße 24, 80331 München, Germany

www.ingramcontent.com/pod-product-compliance
Lightning Source LLC
Chambersburg PA
CBHW071411100726
47908CB00004B/1138

* 9 7 8 1 1 3 8 9 7 1 0 7 3 *